Acclaim for Michael Morwood's
From Sand to Solid Ground

"In a gentle, reassuring and informative way, Michael Morwood responds to the questions that challenge, disturb and sometimes frighten Catholics of our time. He knows the real questions, and the struggles that ensue. He engages the reader in a respectful and inspiring way, and provides background and context so that the questions can be explored in an intelligent and discerning way."

— Diarmuid O'Murchu, author of
Quantum Theology and *Catching Up with Jesus*

"An excellent resource for thinking Catholics caught up in the tectonic shifts of contemporary spiritual change. Morwood has a knack for explaining complex theological ideas in clear, readable prose."

— Joanna Manning, author of *Take Back the Truth*

"*From Sand to Solid Ground* is an extraordinary book of courage and vision. Michael Morwood dares to speak and articulate clearly what more and more Catholics today quietly struggle with and question. His writing exemplifies the giftedness of a true teacher. The book's simple yet elegant style succeeds where perhaps more scholarly, academic theology does not. True teaching not only exposes and explains but inspires and explores as well. Morwood's passionate approach to the faith does all of this and more."

— Barbara Fiand, author of *From Religion Back to Faith*
and *In the Stillness You Will Know*

From Sand to Solid Ground

Questions of Faith for Modern Catholics

MICHAEL MORWOOD

A Crossroad Book
The Crossroad Publishing Company
New York

The Crossroad Publishing Company
16 Penn Plaza – 481 Eighth Avenue, Suite 1550
New York, NY 10001

Printed in the United States of America on acid-free paper

The text of this book is set in 11/16 Galliard.

Library of Congress Cataloging-in-Publication Data
Morwood, Michael.
   From sand to solid ground : questions of faith for modern
Catholics / Michael Morwood.
      p. cm.
   Includes bibliographical references.
   ISBN-13: 978-0-8245-2451-7 (alk. paper)
   ISBN-10: 0-8245-2451-9 (alk. paper)
   1. Catholic Church – Doctrines. 2. Theology, Doctrinal –
Popular works.   I. Title.
   BX1751.3.M68 2006
   230′.2 – dc22
                                                            2006035948

1 2 3 4 5 6 7 8 9 10   12 11 10 09 08 07

Contents

Introduction

We are living through the greatest shift ever in Christian thought. New images of our universe and our planet, along with knowledge about the long, slow development of life on this planet provide us with a new context in which to understand the divine presence we call God always present and active everywhere. Reflection on the universality of this presence leads to further reflection on and a renewed appreciation of Jesus as revealer of this mysterious presence in our everyday living and loving, rather than on Jesus as the mediator between us and a faraway deity. A Church always in need of renewal must engage, at all levels, this shift in images and thought if it is to have integrity and relevance in the twenty-first century.

Attempts at Church renewal in the twentieth century, such as Vatican II in the Roman Catholic Church, took Christians back to the sources of our faith — our Scriptures and early Church practice. Church leadership urged all of us to be involved in this reeducation in the faith in order to appreciate the changes taking place. The result was a groundswell of interest from people in the pews in Scripture, Church history, and basic theology. Many people who participated in this reeducation found themselves wondering why they had not heard so much of it before during an entire lifetime in the Church. They had the consolation of believing that their Church would never keep them in the dark again. They clearly heard that this was a time of openness to and engagement with the modern world. Roman Catholics heard their Church publicly express its need to be always open to reform.

The challenge facing the Catholic Church in the Vatican II period was tremendous, but the challenge facing the Catholic Church — and all of Christianity — in ongoing reform today is much greater and more foundational than any of the challenges faced in that earlier time. It is the challenge to examine the notion of God that underpins Scripture, the Church's doctrine, the Church's identity and its teaching on "salvation," the sacraments, liturgy, prayer, and all aspects of Church life. This challenge was not evident during Vatican II, which did not question the traditional notion of God. Its reforms were laid on foundations cemented with notions that had prevailed throughout Christian history of an elsewhere God overseeing the universe. In these times, however, it is becoming increasingly apparent that this notion of an elsewhere God, so long deemed to be solid rock on which to construct immovable and unchanging doctrine as well as an understanding of the Church's identity, is actually more like shifting sand. It is a primitive concept of God unable to withstand the strong winds of twenty-first-century data and examination. The crux of genuine Church renewal is not about changing

Church policy and teaching on various issues. It is about the concept of God that the Church, at all levels, will use to engage minds and hearts in the twenty-first century. The challenge is inescapable. The door has been opened, and many Christians have walked through to examine their understanding of God and the basics of their Christian faith in perspectives unknown — indeed, unimaginable — a century ago.

In the Catholic Church, the reluctance of institutional leadership to engage this particular challenge has slowed and even retarded the renewal movement begun at Vatican II. Many commentators write and speak of Catholic Church leadership in Rome and throughout the hierarchy as "conservative." "Defensive" and "fearful" could also be used, since there is little doubt that Church leadership is alarmed at the prospect of open examination and discussion of the notion of God that not only underpins Church doctrine but also anchors ecclesial identity and authority. The significant movement in recent years throughout the Catholic Church to control speakers and writers on faith issues is a direct consequence of that fear.

This book is written for readers interested in exploring this challenge facing not only the Catholic Church but all Christian denominations today. It presents a historical overview of the Church's choice of a particular understanding of God and "salvation" for its own ends, at the expense of ignoring Jesus' clear teaching about God's presence with anyone who lives lovingly. History reveals how and why Catholic Church leadership, locked into a narrow theological concept of salvation, is currently fearful and unwilling to allow genuine renewal to progress. A renewed focus on Jesus' teaching concerning the connection between living in love and living in God — and an understanding of God beyond the narrow limits imposed by traditional doctrinal thought — reveal how genuine renewal can occur in the Church.

The Church existed a long time before it became "Catholic" and "Protestant." The central issues raised in this book, our understanding of God, Jesus as revealer of God, and the Church as the community continuing the work of Jesus in the world, embrace what Christians have in common. The various Christian denominations, as institutional entities, have their own ways of responding or not responding to the challenges raised by contemporary study of these basic issues. The book presents the refusal of Roman Catholic institutional leadership to engage the challenges. The rationale for this refusal is explored not just for the sake of renewal within the Roman Catholic Church but also with the hope that it may promote open, honest discussion among Christians of all denominations in our common membership in "the Church."

Jesus clearly preached the good news of God's loving presence to be discovered in the everyday experiences of sharing and of being neighbor. By the time John's Gospel was written decades after Jesus' death the focus in the Christian community had changed to Jesus being the "way" to God, as if no one could have access to God without faith in Jesus. Within four hundred years of Jesus' death, the Christian Church virtually rejected Jesus' understanding that living in love went hand in hand with living in God. It opted instead to teach that everyone was born into a state of utter separation from God. Only baptism into the Christian Church could guarantee access to God. Living in love outside the Church seemingly had no links with God whatever. This distortion of the original teaching of Jesus is the source of what may be termed "ruinous" paths taken by the Church throughout the centuries when it imposed its monopoly on God's presence on the world at large and ruthlessly condemned anyone who dared think outside the parameters of its theological mind-set. Reflection on these ruinous paths can lead us to awareness of the corrective needed for genuine Church renewal: a return to Jesus' teaching that the divine presence cannot be monopolized by institutional religion.

Our world desperately needs religious imagery, concepts, and language that draw people together. Jesus provided all that. The Christian Church, however, has given us theological concepts and imagery that are elitist, exclusive, and divisive. Genuine Church renewal is no longer just for the sake of the Church community. It is now for the sake of the world and the future of humanity. The issue at stake is whether the Church will continue to protect its own unique identity as the "way" to God or whether it will be courageous enough to die to its exclusive claims for the sake of embracing a world in which the divine presence comes to expression in many shapes and forms.

The questions and comments in bold type throughout the text present typical questions and comments raised in adult faith development sessions in which a wide range of views and beliefs is often encountered. People in the pews have a way of cutting through theological jargon and getting to the point. They challenge speakers who would hide behind "Churchspeak" or behind the precise and often convoluted language used by theologians and Church leaders. They want to know in basic terms what the issues are. They want issues to be addressed honestly and openly. They want to know how they arrived at where they are in their thinking and in their practice of the faith. This book attempts to respond to their questions and comments in clear, direct, and uncomplicated language.

The people asking these questions, raising issues, and wanting them to be discussed openly are part of a new phenomenon in the Catholic Church: an informed laity wanting to explore what they believe and why they believe it. These are the people who will ultimately force the institution to renew itself because they will bring questions and issues pertaining to the basics of Christian faith out into the open in a way forbidden to the Church's theologians.

Several patterns are clearly emerging as this public questioning and discussion of foundational faith issues occur. First, people can find themselves being demonized by other Christians who think their questioning is undermining the Church. Questioners can find themselves being charged with disloyalty or with not belonging. Friendships within a faith community can be ruptured. It is not a comfortable position to be in.

Second, people find themselves out of step with the worshiping community because the liturgical language and imagery as well as the preaching no longer nourish or resonate with their journey in faith. This highlights the need for small groups in which faith sharing and ritual can nourish and support adult faith development.

Third, on the positive side, there is an overwhelming sense of relief as people discover they are not alone in their thinking. The joy of this discovery crosses denominational boundaries as Christians find themselves united in exploring basic issues of belief and in ritualizing their shared commitment to being the "body" of Christ.

The significance and importance of this phenomenon is that future generations of Christians will thank these people for being bold enough to face challenges that need to be faced and for shaping Christian belief and practice in ways that can withstand the scrutiny and examination of twenty-first-century data, ideas, and thought. These are the people articulating solid ground on which future generations of Christians can stand with confidence.

Chapter 1

The Elsewhere God

? My children were all educated at Catholic schools, married in the Catholic Church, confess to being "Catholics," have had their children baptized and have them attending Catholic schools, yet they no longer attend Mass and seem quite dismissive of much of what they were taught as Catholics. What is going on?

Whatever is "going on" is going on everywhere in the Western world. In Australia, for example, research indicates that 95 percent of students educated in Catholic schools have no regular participation in Catholic worship within twelve months of leaving school. In the United States 90 percent of Catholics believe they can dissent from Church doctrine and still remain good Catholics. In England, Ireland, and across Europe regular attendance at Sunday worship has dropped dramatically.

? I've heard that one of the main reasons for the dissent and lack of interest is that Catholics are not being sufficiently grounded in the basics of the faith and that the Catholic education system is letting us down.

Many people think so. They think teachers are not teaching clearly the basics of Catholic belief. They insist Catholic schools implement clearer and firmer guidelines that reflect Church teaching as contained in the official *Catechism of the Catholic Church.*

On the other hand, even if this were to happen, as it has in various dioceses, any difference in outcome would be barely discernible.

Basically we are dealing with disbelief, and this disbelief is not confined to Catholics. It is a phenomenon most Christian churches are facing. The adequate response to disbelief is not official or authoritarian insistence on acceptance of what is not believed anymore. That is the heart of the problem. Young people, for example, are ready to believe in "God" but not in terms of a divine being up in the sky somewhere or a God who picks and chooses some people and not others to be his "own" people. They also know enough about the slow development of life on earth to recognize that any religion asking them to believe that the human species suddenly appeared in "paradise" is asking them to perform mental gymnastics. They are too honest to do that anymore.

 Are you saying the Bible story of creation and Adam's sin in the Garden of Eden is not true?

Of course it is not true, if by "true" is meant factual. The human species did not emerge into a state of paradise. Children in the third grade know the dinosaurs died out sixty million years before the human species emerged.

They also know about Ice Ages and other times of mass destruction and annihilation on this planet indicating that the human species emerged into a tough environment.

The Bible stories of creation were written at a time in history when people did not have our knowledge about the development of life on earth. The stories were written with a particular image of God in mind, one that need not be ours today. They are stories addressed to people at a particular time in history with their worldview and the religious questions that emerged from that worldview and their notions about God. In this context the stories conveyed both hope and "truth" for them. But they cannot and should not be taught as literal "fact" today. And most of all, they should not be used, as they are in the *Catechism of the Catholic Church* and in some religious education manuals, as the foundation for our understanding of our relationship with God.

So faith can survive letting go of literal belief in these stories, can it?

Yes. Definitely, unless you choose to believe that the stories in the Bible come directly from God and were intended to tell people for all time just what happened at the beginning of creation. If that belief shapes people's approach to the Bible, they are generally unwilling, on religious grounds, to consider any scientific evidence that might contradict the biblical stories. However, if we understand the stories to emerge from the Spirit of God working in and through the thought patterns, the knowledge available,

17

the worldview at the time, and the questions with which people in that time long ago were struggling for answers, then we are in a position to understand the stories as a means to an end — to give understanding and hope — and not feel bound to read them as factual.

 What I find difficult is that even though I no longer believe the stories literally, the images and thought patterns I acquired from them are extremely difficult to shake off.

That is not surprising, considering the certainty in which we were instructed combined with the constant reference to the stories in a literal fashion in the Church's official liturgy. Both the storytelling and the liturgy have locked popular imagination into images of an elsewhere God who "locked the gates of heaven" and virtually declared that no one would "get in" because the first human being on this planet made a bad mistake. It's hard not to imagine, when we hear the traditional Christian telling of the fall, a localized deity somewhere in outer space reacting and then thinking up a "plan" to fix up what went wrong.

The images linger on in our everyday imagination. How do we imagine God "hears" our prayers? Where does the hearing take place? Most of us carry a lifelong belief that God notices whether we worship or not. Where is the noticing taking place? Questions like these can help us be more aware of the way we imagine God to be like a "person" somewhere, thinking and noticing and planning. And if that is what we are imagining, the time has come for us to question how primitive naïve, and human our image of God is — and the extent to which the Bible stories still impact on our imagination.

I know I've carried those images for most of my life. A male God in heaven who would not let anyone into heaven until Jesus was raised from the dead — a God who notices and keeps a record of my sins.

Precisely. And do we adults ever ask or explore where these images came from? Do we ever reflect on the fact that the popular image of God many of us have carried into our adult life is extremely primitive and outmoded, and lacks credibility when considered in the light of contemporary knowledge about our universe?

That sounds rather sweeping. I know my images of God are only pointers to whom or what God is. Those images work for me and, I am sure, do so for many Christians. We do not really believe that God is like an old man up in the sky somewhere. We recognize that God is beyond our imagination and our ideas. I think our awareness of this prevents us from having an "outmoded" understanding of God or that the God in whom we believe lacks credibility.

In one way that's fine, since all of us will probably end up relating with God according to how we want to shape our image of God or according to how the image has been shaped for us. But we need to consider the elements in the traditional Christian understanding and imagining of God that are in fact extremely primitive and outmoded.

 Such as?

Such as a God who essentially lives somewhere else, who looks down on or over us, who intervenes when "he" wants to, who chooses some people to be "his own," who gets angry, who hands down laws from on high, who demands to be worshiped and takes note if the worship is not given, who keeps a record of wrongdoing, who punishes, who cut off the whole human race from access to "him" because of the fault of one person, who plays favorites, and generally acts much like a tribal lord protecting his interests. This God knows everything, can do anything, and has a "will," a "design" for every person — all mapped out. Some people are even "chosen" to be saved while the rest of humanity is doomed.

All this and more of what we have taken on during our Christian conditioning points to an operating notion of God that is divisive and ruinous. Religions operating with this notion — and Christianity is in the forefront — have not hesitated to wage war and persecute and torture people in the name of this God. This notion of God sets up Christianity, for example, as an elitist religious organization with claims to exclusive access to God. It does this at the expense of recognizing God's presence everywhere, in all people, at all times.

20

But the Christian religion recognizes that God is everywhere. That is one of the first things I ever learned about God.

Yes, it is probably the first thing most of us learned about God. But consider how that understanding of God's presence faded into the background as we were taught the story of the fall and how humankind lost access to heaven. The everywhere God gave way to the elsewhere God, in heaven, a God who locked us out. And Christian doctrine is essentially based on this primitive notion of a Superbeing in heaven who would not let us in.

I'm wondering what a focus on what you are calling the "everywhere God" does to God being "personal."

I think our typical defense of God being "personal" has only added to the perception of the elsewhere, localized Superbeing. We think of "person" as an individual located somewhere, and we have created our typical notion of God as Someone, much like a superhuman person. God hears, God notices, God reacts, God loves, God forgives. There is doubtless something in our human psyche that resonates with, relates with, or even needs this notion of a Person God. God personally loves me. God personally asks me to carry this burden. God spoke to me. God knows me. God has a plan for me. And on the big canvas, God knows everything and has everything in control, so even if some things seem senseless now, God's purpose and plan will one day be revealed. All this helps to give meaning to life and brings much comfort and security to many Christians.

But if we question the notion of a personal God, what are we left with?

We are left with an even greater, much grander, more wonderful, and more awesome Mystery, and we are also left with a far more wonderful appreciation of who and what we are.

God remains the mysterious reality that sustains everything in existence and holds everything in relationship and connectedness — and more. And our knowledge of this expanding universe along with the possibility of other universes deepens awe and respect for this mystery that is beyond all our images.

This mystery is way, way beyond our human personal pronouns. If we want to keep using "personal" language in reference to God, we should do so conscious that we are not describing God. The human concept of "person" undoubtedly helps us greatly to relate with this mystery, but no human concept can adequately contain or describe what God is.

If we forget that — as we constantly do — we idolize a human concept. Worse, we, or the Church establishment, shape the idol to suit our needs.

The language of connectedness, relationship, presence, gift, and trust will probably always be the best language we have to use of our relationship with God, but we need to be wary of constructing an image of God according to human notions of "person" and insisting that is what God is really like.

It seems that the word "God" is itself troublesome since it is so connected, at least in my experience, to an understanding of a supreme being who lives in heaven.

It is a troublesome word, and it would be advantageous either to free it from that connection or to find a substitute title that better honors the ever present, all-pervasive mystery that creates and sustains everything in existence. Neither possibility will be easily achieved. Institutional Christianity, as we shall see, is not likely to help us broaden our understanding of "God," and while we might think of a multitude of substitute names, none of them will adequately describe the mystery to which they point.

Can we still say "God loves us"?

Again, our language traps us because it suggests a personal relationship. We could try reflecting on our relationship with God in slightly different ways. For example: I am held in existence by this awesome mystery that holds everything in this vast universe in existence.

Somehow that does not quite move me that way "God loves me" does.

Sure. But let us take it a bit further. What if I reflect: I give human expression to this awesome mystery that holds everything in existence. This mystery comes to expression in me as nowhere else in the universe. I am a life-form in which this mystery can express love, intelligence, joy, and delight. Here, on this planet, this mystery can speak and sing and dance and paint and create—because of the way of coming to visibility that you and I give it.

There is nowhere else, as far as we presently know, in this entire universe that something as wonderful as this happens.

? You are suggesting a significant shift in the way we reflect on our relationship with God, aren't you?

Yes. There are two key aspects in this. The first is the need to stop thinking of "God" as a personal being who acts much like a human person does. I suspect that this challenge will come as a shock to most Christians since most of us have never thought much about this before. We have simply accepted, uncritically, the idea of God we have had for most of our lives.

The second aspect is to give less time and effort to theologizing about God and who or what God is — except to discard ideas about God that are no longer sustainable — and to shift attention to the wonder of who we are. Who are we? What are we? We are a life-form giving whatever "God" is a way of coming to expression! Our reflection, our times of prayer, our times of community worship should focus on deepening our awareness of the wonder of who we are.

? You seem to be making us more important than God.

No. Definitely not. It is more a matter of recognizing that whatever God is, God is beyond being affected by the human species, that God is mystery beyond our thoughts, images, and words, and that it is our responsibility to give the best possible human expression to this mystery.

 Are you saying that prayer is for our sake rather than for God's sake?

Definitely. God has no need of our prayers. The God who needs or demands our prayer and worship is a human construct. Prayer needs to change *us*. It needs to develop a profound sense of awe and respect about the dignity of human life — all human life. Prayer should be more about who and what we are and lead us to accepting the responsibility for who and what we are. We have wonderful language in our religious tradition that speaks of this. We are temples of God's Spirit; we are earthen vessels that hold a treasure. How, then, are we living what we profess to be? How do we relate with our "neighbor"? How do we relate with our planet? How do we view ourselves? How do we make clear we are actively exhibiting "the kingdom of God" in all we do and say?

 And this is not just for Christians?

The language belongs to our Christian tradition, but the reality is universal. Every human person on this planet is sustained in existence by God. To use familiar language, everyone "lives in God" — and God comes to expression in every person in whatever way the circumstances of that person's life allow God to come to human expression.

I believe that, and I know my children believe it. Yet I also know that in believing it I am at odds with what my Church has taught me since childhood.

What comes to mind?

What comes immediately to mind is the idea that baptism makes us "children" of God and gives us God's Spirit — as if all the unbaptized babies in the world are not born with God's Spirit in them.

We could make a long list, I'm sure, of beliefs and practices that conditioned us to think in terms of people being separated from God. And maybe it would be worthwhile to do so just to bring home to us how strongly conditioned we have been to imagine that all throughout their history, until the coming of Jesus, human beings lived in a state of exile from God and that unbaptized people are still in some way disconnected from God.

But it is not just the unbaptized. I would add to the list all the elderly Catholics I have known who have died wondering if they would get to heaven. What has religion done to them if they die anxious about meeting God?

Yes, too many Catholics and other Christians live life as if it were a journey to God, as if heaven is the really important place. And all the time that divine presence is here in the depths of our hearts and in our everyday decent human actions. What a pity to go through life and not be adequately helped by religion to contemplate the wonder of life as a journey in which we are sustained always by God's presence.

?

But that's the reality for me and many of my Catholic friends. I think we were made fearful of being "presumptuous" if we seriously considered we were close to God.

That is quite common among older Catholics. There was a lot of emphasis on getting rid of our faults, improving ourselves, and hoping that by our good deeds and efforts we would get close to God.

?

And all the time God was with us.

It makes us mindful of the Christmas story. We were looking in the wrong places to find the sacred: God could not really be with us in the "stables" of our own lives. We were conditioned to focus on the elsewhere God rather than the everywhere God.

?

So if God is everywhere, there are no "chosen" people? Only people who thought or think they have been chosen?

Precisely. But rather than discard the notion of "chosen" completely, why not expand it to cover everyone? You would have to think this would have a significant impact on the way people of different cultures and religions think of one another and respect one another.

What about "revelation"?

The shift we face today in our thinking is to move from the notion of an external deity who intervened and, according to Christian tradition, finished the process of revelation soon after Jesus died. According to this thinking, Jesus was the final, definitive revelation of God; God has nothing more to reveal after Jesus and the founding of the Christian Church. This thinking makes sense only if it refers to an elsewhere deity plotting and planning, intervening and then deciding "He" has done enough. This is such a primitive and narrow concept of God (albeit very convenient for Christianity!). No, God is everywhere, and this divine presence comes to expression everywhere according to when and how that presence can come to visibility.

 Back in the 1960s we heard a great deal about "salvation history" and "God's plan of salvation" I notice Pope John Paul II often referred to "God's plan" in his speeches. Does God have a plan of salvation?

St. Paul writes of God's "hidden plan" of salvation in chapter 1 of his Letter to the Ephesians. Christian tradition has consistently alluded to this plan of God to demonstrate God's desire to establish, through Jesus, the Christian religion. And in the 1960s there was considerable catechetical focus on God preparing the world through choosing the Hebrew people for the coming of the Savior. The theme is still central to Christian thinking as evident in the speeches of Pope John Paul II and Cardinal Ratzinger before he became Pope Benedict XVI.

For the present, let us keep in mind that "God's plan of salvation" is a theological notion. It arises in the minds of people whose theological starting point is an actual fall from a state of paradise. It develops in the minds of people who conceive of God thinking and planning like a human person thinks and plans. It then lives on, as it has for two thousand years, in the minds of people whose God is an elsewhere presence who oversees, intervenes, and directs events from outside. It has particular importance for people whose minds are locked into notions of separation of heaven and earth and who think the Christian religion has been chosen by God are the pathway between the two.

At the very least, people who write and speak of "God's plan" should be challenged to articulate what their image and understanding of God is and to what extent their belief in this plan rests on the notion that God locked us out of heaven.

 I think I know the answer to this now, but following this line of approach, I take it there are no laws from on high?

No. There is no external deity thinking about or being disturbed by issues such as how meat is to be prepared or what meat can or cannot be eaten or whether women should be touched at the time of menstruation. Elevating laws and mandates that emanate from cultural practice to being "God's will" is a cultural and religious controlling mechanism. It gives religious and cultural leadership power to demand obedience and conformity.

Can we still talk, then, of "God's Spirit" working in people's lives and inspiring them to formulate laws for the good of society?

That raises the question of what we mean by "God's Spirit." It is significant that we often make this leap to invoke "God's Spirit" when we are dealing with a basically human endeavor. Good laws arise from within a community through discussion and regard for what is beneficial for the community. Does this mean we have to invoke "God's Spirit" as the inspirer, as if an extra burst of God's presence somehow enlightened people? No, let us understand our traditional language about inspiration from "God's Spirit" as referring to people giving expression to the mystery we name "God" that always sustains them in existence.

We should expect different religions to enunciate differing norms and practices. That will always be the way, and this will always call for respect.

 Yes, but some of these religious laws seem too silly or even harmful to be "of God" in any shape or form or understanding.

Some are. Some, for example, are the products of male domination and even of twisted male mentality — such as forbidding girls to be educated. These products should serve to remind us that God comes to expression within human limitations — and all religions need to learn this lesson rather than seeing all their religious laws as somehow divinely inspired by an external deity.

One test of authenticity would be whether the laws are working for the betterment of humanity. That is why it is so important to bring to the foreground and focus on what all the great religions have in common.

That could really be quite a challenge for some religions, couldn't it?

Yes, because they are inclined to devise laws to protect the unique identity and authority of the religious institution. The time has come for all religions to think more globally and to think about what is best for all humankind. But some of the most influential religions refuse to do this, preferring instead to hold on to their institutionalized concept that God is with them uniquely and that they have been chosen to bring the rest of humankind into their fold.

It seems, then, on all levels — personal belief, the decline in Church attendance, and the influence of religion on the world — that a common problematic factor is the elsewhere God who chooses only some?

Yes, it is without doubt a key issue in religion today. The elsewhere God theology has been and remains one of the most destructive influences on this planet. Religion could and should be one of the most powerful influences of good in our world. It could be if it grasped and promoted what is common to all people, what connects us — the presence of the reality we Christians call God. But Christianity is a clear example of a religion that missed the point. Instead of focusing on the God in whom we live and move and have our existence, it shifted focus to the next world, the next life, and who has access to it. It ritualized "exile" and "journey to" God language. It highlighted the haves against the have-nots in terms of access to God's Spirit. Within its own ranks it has consistently bickered and persecuted, tortured, silenced, damned, and exiled men and women who dissented from officially approved thinking.

How, or why, then, did Christianity choose to operate with the elsewhere God theology, and why did it take such a strong hold on Christian thinking for so many centuries?

Let us start with the why and when. The interesting aspect of this is that we will see not only the seeds and the growth of a dominating influence on Christian life and practice that needs correction but will see also the seeds of what the corrective direction could be. That corrective direction was clearly in the foreground in Christianity's beginning.

Chapter 2

The Seeds of Christianity

I learned about Jesus at an early age. I think I have learned very well throughout life what the Church teaches about Jesus. Now in later life, there's a question that intrigues me more and more: Who did Jesus think he was?

Jesus probably viewed himself as a lay preacher who wanted to transform the way people thought about themselves in relationship with God and with one another.

But he would have known more about himself than that, surely? The Catholic *Catechism* says he had "fullness of understanding of the eternal plans he had come to reveal." He would have known he was the Son of God incarnate.

Christian tradition, as expressed in the *Catechism,* holds that view, but it is being openly questioned more and more today. It is questioned because the concept of Jesus being God incarnate and the reasons for believing he had to be God incarnate did not emerge until well after he died. That reasoning process is intrinsically dependent on belief in an elsewhere God denying access to Himself because of Adam's sin. Yet it is clear in Jesus' preaching that he did not hold that belief himself. It is clear that he preached to people insisting that they open their hearts and minds to the reality of a loving God with them, not distant from them. Jesus urged people to walk through life in a relationship of intimacy with and absolute trust in their God.

There is an important issue at stake here. Did Jesus "come," as is generally supposed by Christians, to win back access to God, or was his task rather that of leading people to awareness of the presence of the God always with them?

 But the Gospels present Jesus as being the "way" to God, as if access to God is possible only through him — and the Gospels are our best guide to understanding Jesus, aren't they?

The belief that Jesus is the indispensable "way" to God developed after he died. It is a clear theme in John's Gospel.

In a 1984 statement on Scripture and Christology the Pontifical Biblical Commission explicitly states that the Gospels "present theological interpretations" of what Jesus said and did and says this is "especially true of John."

The Gospels are not biographies. They are primarily faith documents, the products of various communities reflecting on the life of Jesus well after his death. Each Gospel also expresses something of the concerns of the community in the way it related the story of Jesus. Each Gospel writer or editor shaped the material to present the developing understanding about Jesus in a particular Christian community. Much of that understanding was not present when Jesus was alive.

John's Gospel took final shape at the end of the first century. Much of its language and imagery and focus are very different from the other Gospels. It is significant that in John's Gospel the writer has Jesus calling attention to his own importance and identity throughout, whereas in the other, earlier, Gospels Jesus never does this. He preaches about God instead. It is significant for two reasons. First, because it makes it highly likely we are not dealing with Jesus' actual words but rather with a developing understanding in the second half of the first century about Jesus. Second, because it means we have to be careful about quoting Jesus' words in this Gospel to prove he knew in his lifetime an understanding that developed only after he died. And Christians have been doing this for many centuries.

 I have read that the words John's Gospel records Jesus speaking at the Last Supper are not his words. I can appreciate that there may be "theological interpretation" about Jesus in these speeches, but it raises some important issues. If these are not the actual words of Jesus, are they "inspired" by the Holy Spirit? And why should we take notice of them if they are not Jesus' own words?

The words in John's Gospel express who Jesus was for a community. As we saw earlier, "inspiration by God's Spirit" is simply a way of acknowledging God's presence in people — all people, at all times, in all places. That presence will come to light according to the thinking, reasoning, and worldview of people of any place at any time. When we read the words in John's Gospel, we are invited to share the faith they articulate about Jesus. However, we have to read them attuned to the worldview of the writers and notice and question when that worldview intrudes.

For example?

A clear example is Jesus saying in chapter 16 that he has to "go" somewhere in order to "send" the "Advocate," the Spirit of God into the world. This is the sort of dualism that exists in the Gospel that we would not want to hold to today — the notion of separation, distance, and God being elsewhere. Likewise, in chapter 14, Jesus makes the statement referred to earlier, "No one can come to the Father except through me." The statement has been used by Christian leaders for two thousand years to "prove" that only through Jesus can people have access to God. In reality the statement belongs to an early Christian community seeking to give itself importance and identity in the world.

How are we to know, then, what Jesus actually said or did?

We could accept what we read at face value until we hear or read scholarly opinion that this portion of text is not what it seems to be at face value. That puts some responsibility on us to be more educated than we are on the formation of our Scriptures. At the very least we should be open to hearing what Scripture scholarship offers us today, since that scholarship will move us well beyond the face-value reading of Scripture to which we are accustomed.

Is it possible to get below the "theological interpretations" and know the real Jesus?

Yes, to some extent, but it is not an easy task. There are some excellent resources, such as Albert Nolan's *Jesus before Christianity* and writers connected with the Jesus Seminar such as Marcus Borg and John Dominic Crossan. One obstacle is that it is not easy to stop thinking about Jesus as a Christian — and he was not a Christian! He was a Jew. He never renounced his Jewish religion. Never. Not even a hint of it. That alone should make us pause and reexamine our Catholic or Christian bias toward thinking of Jesus as a man on a mission from an elsewhere God to found the Catholic Church or a new religion. It should also make us pause about having Jesus think in concepts that we know developed hundreds of years after he died, such as the Christian understanding of God as three persons in one.

I am disturbed by what you are saying. This approach is clearly contradicting the *Catechism of the Catholic Church*'s understanding of Jesus' mission. Why should I believe what you are saying rather than an official Church statement?

Your choice is whether you believe the *Catechism* without question or whether you are really interested in coming to know the human person we know as Jesus. Your choice is also whether you want to keep believing in the idea of God that the *Catechism* seeks to perpetuate or whether you want to critically examine the notion of God you acquired from the Church. The *Catechism* approach that Jesus walked around Jerusalem "knowing the fullness of the Father's plans" takes Jesus out of the human arena. It is a typical lip-service nod to Jesus being human while presenting the end product of Christian theology as a living reality. This product is a theological construct. It never existed in the flesh.

Who, Jesus?

No, the theological construct — the image of Jesus created by theological thinking well after he died. That Jesus is not the Jesus who lived in Nazareth and died in Jerusalem. Yet most of us have been conditioned to think of Jesus walking around Jerusalem knowing he was the Second Person of the Blessed Trinity and knowing exactly what God's "plan" was.

This is a huge shift you are inviting me to make in the way I understand Jesus.

Yes, it is. However, it is not new. It is simply an effort to start with what happened, what was the human experience, and from there deduce what the events and the experience reveal about God coming to expression in the life, teaching, and death of Jesus.

? **I can see that trying to get in touch with that Jesus is not going to be as easy as I thought it might be.**

We have some helps, though. We know he was a preacher with no official standing in his own religion. We know he was not a scholar. He was not a priest. We know he offended some people. We know his message appealed to many people. He healed. He had a dream. Life tested his commitment to his dream. He had extraordinary trust in his God. He died in failure, abandoned by his male friends. And death was not the end of him.

? **I did a course in theology some time ago, and I have shifted from John's Gospel's presentation of Jesus as someone fully in charge and knowing God's plans for him. I have read Nolan's book, but I still have a nagging question: Where did Jesus get his insights?**

That's a great question because of the other questions it raises. Did an elsewhere God inspire him? Was he the human expression of an elsewhere God, radically different as such, from every other human being? Or did an everywhere God come to visible expression in him?

After Jesus' death, Christian reflection and theology developed the elsewhere God understanding, and that understanding prevails today. But what if we shift focus to the everywhere God coming to human expression in Jesus? The Christian understanding of Jesus as someone giving the fullest possible human expression to God remains intact. We can appreciate Jesus as being to religious insight what Mozart was to music or Van Gogh to art or Einstein to science. Asking where Jesus got his insights is like asking where Mozart got his musical genius. And what is the answer? Mozart received his musical genius from God. Jesus received his insight from God. The significant difference in our thinking does not question the notion of God as the source of all gifts, but asks us to examine where we think God is and how God's presence impinges on human life.

Yes, but when anyone takes that approach, the charge is that it is making Jesus merely human.

Isn't that interesting language, "merely" human! That is why we need a far greater sense of awe and wonder in our religion — about ourselves. We are this incredible life-form that allows God to come to expression, and we talk about being "merely human." It's an indicator of how our religion has so put down our human condition. Isn't it time we started to consider seriously that the import of Jesus' life and message was the revelation of God in and with us? Isn't it time Catholics and other Christians seriously got in touch with the wonder of being human through contemplating the life and teaching of Jesus? Why do we want to persist in thinking we are somehow pulling Jesus down, belittling him, when we speak of him being thoroughly human instead of thinking how his teaching about humanity's intrinsic link with the divine presence raises us up?

Raises us up?

Yes. Isn't that what we have always believed Jesus wanted to do in his preaching to people about the presence of

God in their lives? They, like many of us, thought that God was not close to them. They, like many of us, carried notions of an external God who kept an account of sins and inflicted pain and punishment for those sins. They, like many of us, engaged in religious practices of trying to win or buy God's love or God's presence. Jesus called them, and us, into conversion, to change our images and beliefs so that we might be open to the good news of God-with-us in all we do. These aspects of Jesus' preaching are the indispensable seeds of Christianity: God is intimately with us; God is not to be feared; we all give God a way of coming to expression.

In his preaching about the kingdom of God in the earlier Gospels Jesus does not draw attention to himself as someone who came to mend a rupture between God and people. On the contrary, he urges people to open their minds and hearts to the reality of God-with-them in their neighborly actions. It is not a matter of "God has locked you out, and I have to fix things for you," but rather of "God's presence is here among you; turn away from all ideas and images that block your awareness of that sustaining presence."

 Again you are proposing something radically different from Church teaching. The Catholic *Catechism* teaches that Jesus went to his death knowing he was "the Son of God made man": offering his life "in reparation for our disobedience" (no. 614). The Church is clearly teaching that Jesus died for our sins.

41

The notion that Jesus died for our sins is intrinsically tied to the notion of an elsewhere God acting like an offended tribal lord because something went wrong with his plans. The Catholic *Catechism* also states that "the Father handed his Son over to sinners in order to reconcile us with himself" (no. 614). That statement contains much that is no longer believable. Examine its imagery. God somewhere (else!) decides on an action. Why is this action needed? It is needed because the first human person destroyed the state of paradise and lost connectedness with God by his disobedience.

Then, as if asking us to be scriptural fundamentalists is not enough, we are to imagine this God demanding physical suffering as recompense. And it's worse than that. God organized this. God "handed over" his Son, knowing of course, what "sinners" would do to him, "in order" that we might be reconciled with this God. Is it any wonder that a Christian fundamentalist would produce a film depicting Jesus being beaten to a pulp as if this shows how much God loves us? And God *wants, demands, needs* this suffering in order to be satisfied? Should we be surprised that many Christians want nothing to do anymore with this concept of God?

Why did Jesus have to die, then, if it was not for our sins?

Jesus was no different from all of us in that his life came to an end. What is important about the terrible way he died is his commitment to what he believed. He paid the price

42

for standing true to his beliefs. Life, not an external God, tested him, as it tests all of us at some time. What do we really believe when things go wrong? What holds meaning for us? What sustains us? What sense can we make of pain and suffering? What part does the mysterious presence we call God play when life, as it were, pulls us apart and drains us of any consolation and joy?

We Christians have been too accustomed to remove Jesus from this arena of human questioning and the faith it calls for. The *way* Jesus died, in faithfulness to what he believed, not *why* Jesus died is the issue. The way he died in faith inspires us to hold on in faith when life tests us. It inspires us to share his experience. It invites us to enter into his mind, to appreciate the faith that sustained him in darkness: whatever life does to me I will not give up believing that God is ultimately gracious and present here with me. I will not give in to cynicism and isolation and negativity. I will die believing what I preached about walking in absolute trust in God. I do not believe God is a cruel manipulator of the human condition.

The way Jesus died reveals what we often see in people around us in times of suffering — the depth and the strength of the human spirit. And Jesus invites us to name that spirit as the Spirit of God at work in us.

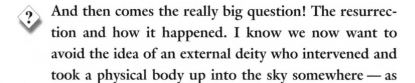 **And then comes the really big question! The resurrection and how it happened. I know we now want to avoid the idea of an external deity who intervened and took a physical body up into the sky somewhere — as**

43

if the Christian religion would crumble if we stopped believing this. How, then, do we talk about what happened to Jesus when he died — and how crucial is what we believe to our Christian faith?

What happens in death is the greatest of all mysteries for us. What is important when speaking about what happened to Jesus when he died is that we stop speaking about it in the worldview of first-century Christians. Jesus did not go "up" to where God really lives. Our existence is *in* God, our dying is *in* God, and whatever happens in death is *in* God. The crucial element of Christian belief about Jesus and whatever happened when he died is that death was not the end of him — not that his body survived and went somewhere. That crucial element sustains us also: death will not be the end of us. We will die *in* God, and however that happens it will involve a transformation to a way of existing rather than a movement to another place.

? It seems Christian preachers are going to have some difficulty with Ascension Thursday then.

It just means that Christian preachers should stop literalizing the Gospel stories about the resurrection of Jesus and appreciate they are stories dealing with mystery. The good news the stories tell — death is not the end of Jesus — should be the focus. This good news is conveyed in story form. Any preacher who insists on belief in the details of the story would be trivializing the mystery which is beyond our images and our concepts.

It would seem that Pentecost is also a mystery dressed up in story form and that we will read the story either through the lens of the elsewhere God or the everywhere God perspective.

Yes, the New Testament writers presented Pentecost in terms of the Spirit coming "down" from elsewhere, like a first-time event. They also presented the Spirit's coming as being dependent on Jesus' resurrection and his ascent into heaven. This made eminent sense to them and fit with their understanding of the cosmos and God's place in it.

Alternatively, if we reflect on Pentecost in terms of God being always and everywhere present and active on earth, then God's "Spirit" has always been here. Let us remember we are not now talking about the "Spirit" as a separate "person" in God. No, let us understand "God's Spirit" or "the Spirit of God" as the influence of that basic, sustaining mystery that holds everything in existence — God. From the planet's beginning, God's Spirit has come to visibility in and through whatever was there to work with. This continued with the emergence of the human species. All its development took place *in* God, giving God a way of coming to expression in the magnificent life-form we are and could yet be. Late in its development this life-form came to serious reflection about itself, its place on this planet, and whatever sustained it in existence. This was done slowly and tentatively as human minds in various parts of the planet grappled with questions of meaning, purpose, and connectedness. And all the time the Spirit of God was present and active in them, coming to expression in and

45

limited by the knowledge and the worldview of the time as well as the personal giftedness of the thinkers. Gradually religion became an important factor for the human species because religion attempted to give answers to these questions.

We can imagine the Spirit of God active in all parts of the world coming to expression in the great religious leaders. Then, in Jesus of Nazareth, the same Spirit burst forth in someone gifted enough to give that Spirit extraordinary expression both by the way he lived and by what he taught.

This same Spirit was always present and active in all the people Jesus addressed. The Spirit was always present and active in the apostles — but limited by the religious conditioning, by the lived situation, by individual personalities, and by images and ideas that told these people God was not with the likes of them.

It was not till after the death of Jesus that the Aha! moment dawned, when minds were opened — by thinking about Jesus — and understanding came. Then the Spirit that had always been present in these people was able to come to expression in a new way. But it did not come from somewhere else.

Pentecost has traditionally been linked with the beginning of the Christian Church. Is this still so?

No. Not in the sense of a religion quite separate from the Jewish religion. We know this separation took several generations to occur. The first followers of Jesus were Jews,

and our own Scriptures inform us that they remained faithful as Jews. They visited the temple every day for prayer.
This makes Pentecost even more interesting, doesn't it? It
was a Jewish experience, not a spectacular event that the
Christian religion can claim as its birthday.

**Yes, but surely it set the course for inevitable separa-
tion, and in that sense Christianity can claim it as its
beginning?**

No. The Pentecost experience did not set the course for
inevitable separation. What set the course for separation
was the theological schema that developed after Pentecost
and the way that schema interpreted Jesus according to a
"plan" God had for our salvation.

So was Pentecost intended for Jews only?

Again, no. It happened in a Jewish context, but the crux
of Pentecost was its universality. Think of the Spirit of
God active through all those years of human development,
breaking into wonderful expression here and there around
the world, and then in Jesus, the Jew, it came to such clear,
human expression. His Jewish companions reflected on
what they saw and heard in him and came to a Wow! con-
clusion: look what happens when someone wholeheartedly
allows the Spirit of God to come to expression in him or
her! We see something of the unknowable God. We see
something of the wonder of who we are — temples of
the Spirit of God. We realize our connectedness with *all
people*: everyone who lives lovingly like this lives *in* God

and God lives *in* them. We see how we should live in right relationship with everyone. We see what Jesus meant when he was speaking about the "reign" or the "kingdom" of God among us.

If we could personify the Spirit of God, we could imagine that Spirit saying, "At last! At last they have seen what human life is all about! At last they have seen how everyone is connected! At last they have seen the dignity of all people! At last they have a language and the insight to transcend the religious language of choice, elitism, distance and separation, us and them. At last fear and division are cast out! At last, if this message spreads, all people will know and walk in a trusting and loving relationship with the presence that holds them all in existence."

Pentecost is a great story! The story conveys what could have been the most wonderful breakthrough in human development: a clear articulation of our common connectedness with one another and the Source and Sustainer of all. This story transcends languages, cultures, and religions. This is a story of healings, of breakthroughs in understanding, of what the Spirit of God can do in people when they open their minds and hearts to the power that is within them. This is a universal story, for all people. It set hearts and minds on fire. It was good news. It demanded to be proclaimed as such and to be told over and over again because it would set people free from resorting to magic and superstition and dependence on people with special powers to access the sacred. The sacred was accessible to everyone.

Yet, incredibly, within the space of several hundred years this reading of the story would be neglected and almost abandoned in favor of Christian insistence that a story of separation and exile from God be the story on which its doctrine, its ritual, its prayers, its spirituality, its identity, and its sacramental life be based. This insistence, with its trust in human concepts rather than trust in the universal presence of the Spirit of God, underpins the many ruinous states the Christian religion and, in particular, the Catholic Church, would create throughout the centuries. The hope for the future is to sift through some of the ruins, to learn from the mistakes, and to free the insights of Jesus and Pentecost from the weeds and thorns of a story that has overshadowed and all but strangled them.

Chapter 3

The Destruction of the Good News Story

 If the Pentecost experience, as described here, offered so much to people, why was it abandoned or neglected?

Within several generations of Jesus the Christian religion moved from appreciation of Jesus' inclusive message about God's presence with people to an exclusive, elitist understanding of its own identity. It came to view itself as the sole indispensable source of access to an *elsewhere* God. The more its thinking developed in that direction, the more it lost sight of Jesus' message. It focused instead on articulating a theological schema that established and cemented its unique position among religions.

 Christianity was unique, though, and had every right to proclaim its uniqueness.

Certainly, but the theological schema it adopted changed the uniqueness of its message. If the Church had been faithful to Pentecost it could and would have preached to all people the good news of God-in-their-midst. But that is not what happened. The more the Church established its unique identity, the more it developed and preached a theological understanding that God was *not* with everyone. It preached that only by entry into the Church could people gain access to God.

So thinking and preaching about Jesus also changed?

Yes, and that had a ruinous effect on the Pentecost experience of God's presence. Over the centuries Christians gradually stopped reflecting on Jesus as someone who revealed the wonder and the dignity of men and women as bearers of the sacred. Unbelievably, Jesus became a theological problem. Great minds engaged the problem of who Jesus had to be in order to win access to heaven for us. They considered that no mere mortal human being could do this. They concluded that Jesus *had* to be *more* than human. Only if Jesus was identified as one with God in a way the rest of humanity is not could their notion of Jesus saving us by gaining access to heaven be feasible.

What triggered this radical change of focus from the universal presence of God's Spirit with people to dealing with a theological problem?

We can see the beginnings of the change with Paul's interpretation of Jesus in the scenario we have already discussed: Adam's sin, loss of access to God's dwelling place, everyone before Jesus dying into a state of separation from God, and Jesus by his obedient life fulfilling God's plan to mend what went wrong. This schema created a theological mind-set in which Christian thought became fixated on the elsewhere God and how access is gained to the elsewhere God.

? And the early Church community used this theology to shape its unique identity?

Yes, especially after the community split with Judaism in the second half of the first century. There was not much to be gained, apparently, by proclaiming God's presence with everyone, and much to be gained by claiming that this community, through Jesus and its rituals, had unique access to God.

This institutional movement mirrored the movement of the Hebrew people centuries earlier in proclaiming they were uniquely God's people and in unique covenant with God. The claim gave them special identity, affirmation, purpose, and great heart in times of oppression and difficulty.

? I can appreciate that members of the Church at this time doubtless thought that what they were offering — access to God — was of great benefit to the whole world, but it seems to have come at the cost of ignoring God's presence with all people.

Exactly. The "good news" became more the message of unique access to God than Jesus revealing that everyone had access to God in being neighbor to one another.

How long did it take for this theological thinking to become firmly established within the Christian community?

Amazingly, if we could transport ourselves back to the beginning of the second century, with notions of an everywhere God, that everyone has access to God's presence and enlightenment, that the Spirit that moves in Jesus moves in us, and that we should trust it and see where the Spirit leads — we would be held in suspicion by Church leadership.

The claim to have direct access to God was seen to be subversive of Church authority and order, especially when Clement (writing 90–100) argued that God rules all things and that God has delegated his authority to bishops, priests, and deacons. Anyone who refused to obey them disobeyed God.

Here, so early in Christian history, came the clear division between laity and a controlling hierarchy who must be believed as the voice of God.

Ignatius of Antioch, in Syria, a generation later, went a step further and said the division of bishop, priest, and deacon mirrors a heavenly hierarchy. He taught that the bishop must be obeyed "as if he were God." For Ignatius, God became accessible to humanity through the Church — and its rulers.

About the same time, another famous Church leader, Irenaeus, taught that just as there was one God, so there was only one Church — and the only true representative of God in the community was the bishop.

So Church practice and thinking within a hundred years of Jesus' death canonized a theological schema of salvation that not only made Jesus the unique accessor to God; it also made the institutional Church necessary for access to God.

? Our Creed reflects this thinking about an elsewhere God, doesn't it?

Yes. The Nicaean Creed, which has its roots in the deliberations at the Council of Nicaea in the fourth century, has shaped traditional Christian thought and imagination about God and Jesus. Its focus is the God who lives in heaven. Jesus became a God-person who "came down from heaven" and when he died "ascended into heaven."

It is significant that the Creed says nothing about Jesus as revealer of God among us.

? Why did the Church need to have a Creed?

Bitter arguments over whether Jesus had to be a special incarnation of God in order to win access to heaven erupted throughout the Church. In the fourth century, Athanasius, who represented the liberal side of thinking, argued strongly that unless Jesus was God incarnate we could not be saved. Athanasius was astute enough to realize that this theological position would also grant the Church a unique and strong role in society. On the conservative side, Arius and his followers argued that God used Jesus' humanity to save us. They wanted to preserve traditional belief in God's Otherness and saw no need to elevate Jesus

54

to being identified in some way with God. They thought that doing so was offensive to God.

Disagreements on this crucial topic of Christian faith inflamed tempers in some towns and resulted in fighting in the streets. Emperor Constantine was not at all pleased to see his efforts to maintain a peaceful empire being disturbed by Christians fighting over theological differences. His concern for civil peace prompted him to host 250 bishops from the East at his summer residence at Nicaea in 325 and order them to come to some agreement. Athanasius and his followers, with considerable support from Constantine, won the debate at Nicaea, and the Nicaean Creed reflects their beliefs.

The Creed that eventually resulted was needed not only to clarify doctrinal issues. It was needed, demanded even, by the emperor as a means of ending civil unrest.

 Why did the emperor host the council and not the pope?

Papal control over all the Church had not yet been established. The pope was not present at this council. The Council of Nicaea was a gathering of Eastern, Greek-speaking bishops with only a representative from Rome present. In the first thousand years of Christian history no pope ever convened a general council of the Church.

Constantine's power and authority far exceeded that of any Church leader, and he exercised that authority in Church affairs. It was Constantine who made Sunday the day of rest. He made Christmas a feast by joining it with the pagan feast of the sun's birthday on December 25. He favored the advancement of Christians in the public service and helped them become the wealthy ruling class. He made the clerical state an attractive proposition by granting it privileges and exemptions. He had great basilicas built in Rome and Jerusalem. He even participated in the debates at Nicaea. The emperor, not the pope, was the power broker.

The council at Nicaea did not end the disagreements, though, did it? Thirty-four years later another, even larger council of the Church, with five hundred bishops from both the East and the West overturned the doctrinal statements of Nicaea and sided with Arius. So the debate continued.

Christians rarely hear of that council at Rimini-Seleucia, doubtless because it is an embarrassment to a Church that believes its councils cannot make mistakes. When Constantine died, his son Constantius became ruler in 350. His strong support for the Arian position and his persecution of supporters of the Nicaean Creed made this council possible.

It says something about the human nature of Church councils that two of them, a little more than a generation apart, could reach such diametrically opposed conclusions. It could serve as a warning not to declare the decisions of any council as the final word on any subject.

But Christianity eventually returned to and accepted Nicaea's statements as binding and has clearly asserted ever since that Arius was wrong.

While that is true, there was another, but little-known, factor that was decisive in the turnaround. When Theodosius became emperor toward the end of the fourth century, he decreed that everyone must become Christian under pain of being judged "demented or insane." Those who refused to do so were banned from meeting in public and were threatened with punishment by imperial edict. The Nicaean doctrines were imposed on everyone. This marked a significant shift in Christianity: the use of force and punishment to ensure acceptance of official Church teaching. The tactic became a feature of Church leadership throughout the centuries to silence questioning of doctrinal statements.

This is a long way removed from the spirit of Pentecost and from the manner in which Jesus preached.

 I have always regarded the Creed as unquestionable. It's almost like God wrote it — well, at least inspiring the men at Nicaea so that there could be no mistake. Now I'm hearing it is more a human document elevated to divine status. Is this a fair comment?

The most significant factor about the Creed today is that it is the answer to a question that is totally irrelevant to many Christians: who does Jesus have to be in order to gain access to God after Adam sinned? The historical context of the Creed indicates it is no more and no less than what brilliant men, with particular concerns, can produce at a particular time in history, in the worldview of the time, in response to questions arising from that particular world-view. If we could see it this way we could avoid in the future some of the ruins that litter Church history when councils, supposedly articulating "eternal truths" in God's name, have made statements that merely reflect attitudes and thought patterns of the time.

 That contradicts the clear teaching of the Church that says faith is certain knowledge. The *Catechism of the Catholic Church* states, "Faith is *certain*. It is more certain than all human knowledge, because it is founded on the very word of God who cannot lie" (no. 157; emphasis in original text).

In adopting such an extreme measure the institutional Church has backed itself into a corner. Faith, as expressed in the Creed, must then rest on the *certainty* of an actual "fall." The Creed assumes this *was* the actual situation; these *were* its consequences; this is *how* the ruptured relationship with God was repaired; and this is *who* Jesus had to be in order to accomplish this. This creedal worldview is then used to give the Church its special, elite identity and role in the world. Institutional Church leadership then finds itself in the corner, defensive, fighting against or protecting itself from any data, development, or knowledge that suggests an actual fall is far from "certain" or that God actually lives in a place called heaven. This is why we should not be surprised that Church leadership has ensured that the Creed is off limits for questioning or criticism.

Wouldn't you agree, though, that some aspects of Christian faith — original sin, for example — are certain? While some may question the certainty of a fall, surely the reality of original sin is beyond doubt. We only have to look around us and see its effects.

That will depend on how we understand "original sin." If it means that the human species is imperfect insofar as its members are all capable of making mistakes, then the evidence is compelling. However, if it means, as traditional Christian teaching wants us to believe, that this imperfection stems from a mistake made by the first member of the human species, then the only evidence is a biblical story that was never intended to be a scientific account of human beginnings. The *Catechism of the Catholic Church*, however, states that the account in Genesis "uses figurative language but affirms a primeval event that took place at the beginning of the history of man" (no. 390). To insist that Catholics believe this is to insist that they ignore the wealth of evidence to the contrary. That sort of faith is not "certain." It is faith afraid of embracing new information. A theological schema of salvation built on this foundation is unable to withstand contemporary scrutiny and will inevitably crumble.

 I've always had trouble believing that everyone is born into a state of separation from God. I've never really thought that Jesus believed this either.

It is not the picture Jesus gave when he embraced children or when he spoke to the "crowd," the down-and-outs of society, is it? It is clear that Jesus did not approach children and adults with the view that God was not with them. On the contrary, he urged them to open their eyes and their minds to the reality of God's presence with them.

The Celts also did not believe human nature was tainted in the way St. Augustine taught. There seems to be a great interest today in "Celtic spirituality." Can it be a corrective to the course Christianity took with its focus on original sin?

Definitely. The most famous Celtic voice at the time of Augustine was a layman from Britain, Pelagius. He was fluent in Latin and Greek and well-known for his knowledge of the Bible and for his preaching. He arrived in Rome in 382, not long before Rome was to fall to barbarian forces. He was shocked by both the pessimism and the lack of morality in the city. He preached an encouraging Christian message: creation is good; human nature is good; there is hope of revival because sin and its effects can be overcome. He presented the Celtic view that all things are interconnected in God and that renewal and "salvation" could come through cooperation with one another. He never denied the need for God's help (grace) while stressing the human response.

I've heard of the "Pelagian heresy." Is this the man to whom it refers and, if so, what was the heresy?

Pelagius ran afoul of Augustine and other powerful forces in the Church, mainly because he was denying Augustine's teaching that human nature was depraved because of Adam's sin. The "heresy" is really a caricature of Pelagius's thinking, as if Pelagius taught that human beings can act without any need of God's help. Pelagius never taught that.

? Since Augustine's teaching on original sin has been the cornerstone of much of Christian theology for centuries, I guess it made sense to silence a contrary voice.

There is a sentence in the *Catechism of the Catholic Church* that highlights the dilemma faced then and now by the Church: "The Church, which has the mind of Christ, knows very well that we cannot tamper with the revelation of Original Sin without undermining the mystery of Christ" (no. 389).

In other words, what do we do with our doctrine about Jesus as the one who attains a place in heaven for us if we tamper with the belief that God locked us out?

? What amazes me more than anything else is that by the end of the fourth century our Church accepted the belief that everyone born into the world is born into a state of separation from God — and needs baptism to gain connection with God. Yet fundamentally this belief indicates that Jesus was wrong! It insinuates that the "kingdom" of God, God's presence, is not found in neighborly love for one another.

It was quite a significant shift, a far cry from the Pentecost insight. Christian belief now held, for example, that if someone in Outer Mongolia lived a life of extraordinary love and generosity, he or she could not be living in God nor could God be living in that person. God's presence could come only through the sacrament of baptism.

? **I'm wondering now what might have happened if Christianity had not deviated into doctrinal definitions concerned with access to an elsewhere God and had been more faithful to the inclusive, God-with-us Pentecost experience.**

We will never know just how differently both the Church and society may have been shaped if the Church had stayed focused on Jesus' preaching about God-with-us in our everyday actions. Granted the direction the Church took, though, a surprising possibility emerges — that Jesus may have been far more at home with the developments in his Jewish religion than with those within the Christian community of the Nicaean era.

In *The History of God,* Karen Armstrong records the development in the Jewish community after the fall of Jerusalem and the destruction of the Temple in the first century of the Christian era. The Pharisees, a lay group, urged members of the Jewish community to believe they were a holy people. They taught that God is present to all; God is present without the need of a priestly caste. They urged cleansing and ritual purity — not for the sake of winning God's approval or presence, but as a way of expressing or acknowledging their own sacredness.

During the next four centuries, while the Christian community was bitterly divided over theological problems concerning an elsewhere God, Jewish scholars worked on the understanding that God was not to be thought of as a "Big Brother, watching their every move from above" and that Jews "were to cultivate a sense of God within each human being so that our dealings with others become sacred encounters."[1] The scholars considered it was far more important to cultivate this sense of God's presence with people rather than "find neat solutions."[2]

Jesus may well have been more at home with the Jewish scholars than with Athanasius and Arius, the theological deliberations at Nicaea and Augustine's insistence on "original sin."

That is truly ironic! The Pharisees and rabbis were closer to what Jesus preached about the kingdom of God in our midst than the Christians! Then the Christians turned on them and persecuted them in the name of the elsewhere God the Christians had come to idolize.

To make matters worse, while the Pharisees, a lay group, and the Jewish rabbis were intent on affirming God's closeness with people, the Christian priesthood changed quite radically. Priests became set apart from people, and liturgy became more cultic because of the influence of both pagan and Old Testament cultic notions of priesthood. These notions highlighted the role of the priest as someone with special powers to access the arena of the sacred.

Previously, the lifestyle of priests was similar to that of most laypeople. They married and had full-time jobs. During Constantine's reign, when they were paid for their priestly work and gained special privileges, they began to withdraw more and more from secular occupations and became a group apart from ordinary people. Historians point out that before Constantine the Church considered itself the realm of the sacred opposed to a profane world. Constantine's reign broke down this division and replaced it with that between the sacred clergy and the profane people. This division was accentuated with the idea that sexual intercourse was not in keeping with the priestly character.

 And after Augustine, in the fifth century, the doctrine of original sin radically changed the sacrament of baptism?

Yes. In the first centuries, baptism was basically an adult ritual symbolizing a person's readiness to stand up and be counted as a Christian, as someone in whose life the mind and Spirit seen in Jesus' life would be evident. It was like standing before the community and proclaiming, "I know the Spirit that moved in Jesus wants to move in my life. I give you my word: you will see this Spirit operating in all I do and say. Immerse me in water as a sign of my total commitment to allowing the Spirit to lead me — just as Jesus did at his baptism." In its early form, baptism was not a ritual concerned with distance from God. It was a ritual that affirmed people as bearers of the Spirit of God and called them to witness to that Spirit.

The sacrament changed dramatically in the fifth century when the notion of everyone being born into a state of separation from God became the dominant Christian worldview. Thereafter, baptism came to be understood as a ritual that "cleansed" people from original sin and made them "children of God" and "members of His Church." At a time of a high infant mortality, this thinking led to an emphasis on baptizing babies out of concern for getting them "into heaven."

The practice of infant baptism, like the mass conversion of pagans during Constantine's rule, helped to produce a body of faithful who were not personally committed to the Church. The impact on Church life was significant.

Understanding baptism primarily as the removal of original sin also strengthened belief that membership of the Church was the only way anyone could "be saved." God, in this theological schema, was definitely not present to unbaptized people.

 What happened to eucharistic participation once the theology of original sin became paramount?

St. Augustine spoke eloquently to the new members of the Church about to receive Communion for the first time on the night of their baptism. They were to understand that Christians are "the Body of Christ." Their "Amen" when hearing the minister say, "The Body of Christ," and receiving the consecrated bread in their hands was to be their way of saying "Yes" to who they were. Augustine urged the newcomers and all Christians to "be" what they were receiving.

Five hundred years later, however, about the year 1000, the Christian faithful were not going to Communion. Not only were they not going, it had become inconceivable for them to think of themselves in the way Augustine had exhorted his listeners. Instead, centuries of preaching and Church practice molded by the "original sin" fixation had produced a Christian faithful immersed in notions of unworthiness, separation from God, guilt, and fear of God.

This historical reality indicates the ruinous effects of a theological schema at odds with the preaching of Jesus and the insights of Pentecost. People did not consider themselves to be "temples of God's Spirit." Instead, they were the banished children of Eve. They were exiles from God. They did not believe in themselves as a sacred "body." They were sinners, and very few of them believed they had much chance of ever getting to heaven. That is why the notion of purgatory became so popular in the twelfth century. It held out some chance of getting to heaven after a time of purification.

It is hard to believe that within a thousand years of Pentecost, eucharistic practice and devotion became linked with magic and superstition centering on the "sacred object," the consecrated host, which the people could no longer touch but could only look at and adore from a distance.

It is hard to believe that the Christian community would build screens in churches to separate people from the "sacred space" where the priest officiated.

It is hard to believe that the Christian religion would become characterized by fear of God and God's stern judgment on people, with many churches featuring fearful images of Jesus sitting in judgment and the torments of those damned to hell.

 It seems to have been a characteristic of my (older) generation of Catholics that we have carried throughout our lives rather fearful images of being judged when we die. We were taught not to presume we would get to heaven and have carried all our lives a sense of not knowing or not being sure whether we will get into heaven.

What a drawback that has been to a healthy Catholic outlook on life and death. We have the "Depart from me . . ." words ringing in our ears. We have been led to imagine a judgment after death when God will go through our lives minute by minute, weigh up the good and the bad, then pronounce whether we stand with the sheep or the goats. All of this is a sad, sorry, and primitive notion of God and a distortion of Jesus' parable about sheep and goats. Who are the sheep? The "sheep," are people who do the everyday family and neighborly deeds of feeding, clothing, visiting, and caring. Who are the goats? The "goats" are people who *never* do these deeds. "Never" is a strong word. We will live and die as "sheep," or we will live and die as "goats." The matter will not be decided after we die. And all of us ought to be confident that we are on the sheep side. It is amazing that a parable that should reassure people living decent lives has been turned into a parable to put the fear of God into people and have them anxious about meeting God when they die.

What a dramatic change from those first years of Christian life when people of all walks of life gathered to break bread, to celebrate the good news of life's journey with their God, to rejoice in God's graciousness and to pledge their willingness to act as bearers of the sacred.

 Some of us are old enough to remember we were never allowed to touch the host at Mass. Our understanding was that the host was sacred; we were not. We also heard a lot about "transubstantiation" as an explanation of how the consecration at Mass worked. I've never really understood it, and I suspect most Catholics do not understand it either. Why did Church scholarship concern itself with how the sacrament worked rather than focusing on what it was meant to celebrate?

In the eleventh and twelfth centuries questions about eucharistic language and theology became quite controversial. The controversy was driven by the desire to understand, to classify, and to organize knowledge into logical systems. Scholars in these centuries sought to understand how Jesus becomes "present" in the consecrated bread. What manner of presence is it? If the presence is not physical, as an actual human body, what is meant by saying it is "real"? Does "real" mean "actual"? Can "actual" or "real" presence be understood by the words, "sacramental presence"? Do we have to say Jesus' presence is "more than symbolic"? If "more than symbolic," what do we mean?

The controversy and confusion were highlighted earlier when a meeting of bishops in Rome in 1059 forced Berengarius of Tours, a theologian, to publicly profess his assent to the teaching of "the Holy Roman Church and the Apostolic See" that "the bread and wine which are placed on the altar are not merely a sacrament after consecration, but are rather the true body and blood of our Lord Jesus Christ—and that these are truly, physically, and not merely sacramentally touched and broken by the hands of the priests and crushed by the teeth of the faithful."

The language "not merely a sacrament" is significant. It signifies a move to "realist" thinking about the Eucharist. "Really and truly" became and remains a phrase to test correct belief among Roman Catholics about the presence of Jesus in the consecrated bread.

"Transubstantiation" became the Church's official answer to questions arising from the realist approach to the consecration. Something must actually happen to the bread for a "real" change to occur after the words of consecration. How can this "real presence" come into what looks like bread? The theory of transubstantiation explained that the bread still looked like bread (outward appearance) but somehow underwent a "substantial" change beneath the outward appearances.

? **Nothing more epitomizes for me the destruction of the promise of Pentecost than to see my Church fixated on how a sacrament "works"! It's like asking how my wedding ring works and having no concern for what it means for me personally.**

Yes, and the mental construct supposedly explaining how a symbol is "more than" a symbol became a statement of faith. As such it also falls into the category of "certain knowledge," beyond questioning. Church authority then insists: this is reality; this is how it works; this is what you must believe if you want to call yourself a Catholic.

This mental construct conditioned Catholics for centuries to believe that the host was "really sacred" and they were not. Eucharistic theology and practice effectively separated the sacred and the human. The sacrament at the heart of Christian life became diametrically opposed to Jesus' preaching and the Pentecost experience.

Attention to the sacred object, the consecrated host, brought exaggerated concern with rubrics and legalism in liturgy. It produced tight centralist (Roman) control over eucharistic practice. It also led to an ever-broadening chasm between the priest (the holy person doing the actions correctly) and the community (passive recipients). The priest did not have to engage the people in the sacramental activity. His primary task was to do the action with the right words and gestures so that the sacrament "worked."

? **We Catholics still carry a strong sense that the priest has special powers we do not have and only he can bring**

the presence of Jesus to the bread at the consecration. There is something about this thinking that makes us dependent still. I wonder how we will ever get over or around this.

We will never do so as long as we continue to understand priesthood and Eucharist in the mind-set of what became "traditional" Catholic theology. We have to move from a focus on the sacred object, how it "works" and who has power to do it, to the proper focus of committing ourselves to *being* the sacred presence for one another. This requires prayers and practices that are inclusive and affirming of God's presence rather than those that condition people to think they are "exiles" on a journey "to" God. We need to celebrate Jesus, not as a go-between, between us and the God who resides in heaven, but as someone who reveals the wonder of God in our midst. We need to be far more explicit about what we are committing ourselves to when we eat and drink together in memory of Jesus.

 I can appreciate there was a dramatic shift in sacramental practice in the Middle Ages, but I think some balance is needed. I think we need to acknowledge that the Middle Ages produced some of the Church's greatest thinkers and saw the growth of universities and the spread of education.

Yes, Thomas Aquinas (1225–74) would still be regarded by many as the greatest scholar of all time in the Church, and his influence in Catholic seminaries over the centuries has been without equal. This was a time of great learning

71

and debate. In Western Europe all education was conducted by the Church. The great thinkers were usually monks or members of the clergy. It was a time when Church scholars, known as the "scholastics," were intent on articulating Christian faith in a logical system. They relied heavily on the teaching of the ancient Greek writer Aristotle, the Bible, and the early Church writers.

The quest to synthesize faith was challenging and exciting. Great minds were at work, and debate was vigorous. On the other hand the scholastic movement led to a significant shift in Church affairs. The intellectual focus on giving precise and logical answers of all aspects of belief and Church practice did little for the faith of people in the pews. It set a direction that lasts till our day — the use of abstract and technical language by academics communicating with other academics. The language of Scholasticism was not the language of everyday faith. It was not language about Jesus, human like us. It was not language about God in our midst. It was not scholarship for the sake of the people. It was scholarship for the sake of scholars. The overall effect was the further diminishment of the good news story in favor of correct thinking.

Yet at the same time the scholastics were deliberating, there were men and women, intent on the good news story, who pushed for Church renewal through a return to Gospel values.

Yes. If we go back to the twelfth century, St. Bernard comes immediately to mind. He founded the Cistercian abbey at Clairvaux and became the great voice of spiritual revival. Before he died in 1153, the Cistercians had founded monasteries in Italy, France, Germany, England, Spain, Ireland, Poland, and Hungary.

St. Francis of Assisi was born late in the twelfth century. His radical witness to Gospel values, especially love, generosity, poverty, and a love of nature inspired many followers.

St. Dominic, the founder of the Dominicans, was a contemporary of Francis. He met with Francis and, while having great respect for Francis's dedication to poverty, placed his emphasis on solid intellectual training as the foundation for good preaching.

The Franciscan and Dominican religious orders, along with the Carmelites and the Augustinians, were a timely new phenomenon in the Church. Whereas the monastic life had stressed a withdrawal from the world, members of these religious orders engaged the world through witness and preaching. They were a timely balance to the world of scholasticism. They were timely also because many people were shifting from villages to the growing towns and risked losing all contact with the Church.

Another phenomenon of the times was women who were visionaries or mystics who had quite an influence on renewal in the Church. Hildegard of Bingen, for example, preached a sermon to the higher clergy of Cologne in 1163. Some of these women must have been quite perplexing to men in positions of control who seemed not too sure whether to listen to them or not.

The fourteenth century produced some very influential women. Bridget of Sweden, pronounced co-patroness of Europe by Pope John Paul II, was married at thirteen, had eight children, and after her husband died devoted her life to Church renewal through the reform of the lives of the pope, bishops, clergy, and secular rulers. Catherine of Siena was confidante of Popes Gregory XI and Urban VI. "Up, father! No more irresponsibility!" she wrote in one letter to Pope Gregory. Legend records that he died regretting he ever listened to "meddling women."

Meanwhile in England, another woman with visionary experiences, Julian of Norwich, wrote of the wonder and the constancy of God's love, a love "that has never abated and never will. . . . In this love our life is everlasting. . . . In this love we have our beginning, and all this we shall see in God without end."

Julian of Norwich called people to put their trust in God's love. This call was particularly significant given that the Church generally at the time was doing anything but that. The Black Death had by the mid-fourteenth century killed about a third of the population of Europe. In one three-month period half the population of Florence was wiped out. The notion that the plague was God's punishment for a wicked world seemed a reasonable explanation, one in keeping with Christianity's notion of a God who keeps a record of wrongdoing and punishes accordingly.

The idea of God punishing was even stronger at the time Julian was writing, when for a period of thirty-five years the Church was in schism, with several popes claiming to be the true pope. Monks and clergy preached that this division in the Church was also a form of God's punishment.

 The concept of a punishing God seems so far removed from what Jesus preached. What strikes me as really odd is that St. Anselm in the late eleventh century popularized the idea of Jesus' death paying off the debt that humanity owed to God because of its sinfulness. But it seems that even this was not enough. At the time of the Black Plague the concept of a God still intent on dreadful punishment held sway throughout the Christian world. This is a God who will never let up, isn't it?

And how many Christians in our times still carry this image of an elsewhere God brooding over the world and inflicting punishment when things do not go according to his "plan"!

Christianity will never be able to renew itself to any worthwhile degree as long as this elsewhere God is idolized and worshiped. How can you genuinely reform a Church if your reforming movement is grounded in the concept of an elsewhere God, watchful, strict, interventionist, and ready to punish unbelievers? How can you reform a Church when the experience of Pentecost has been replaced with human, theological constructs, and even the reforming Christians believe they cannot think outside the narrow parameters of that theology?

The destruction of the good news and the distortion of the Pentecost experience would appall Jesus. Over the centuries he was effectively removed from people as a companion and friend, as someone with whom they could share the burdens of their own lives, heart speaking to heart. Even worse, everything he wanted people to believe about walking in a trusting relationship with their God was smothered in the original-sin mind-set that told people they were intrinsically evil. The God that Jesus longed for people to know was replaced with a fearful, judgmental deity prone to inflict dreadful punishments on sinful humanity.

Very few Christians could presume to walk in peace all the days of their lives with this God. The Church's sacramental system no longer symbolized the wonder of God's presence with people.

There are three issues foundational to Jesus' preaching about the "kingdom" of God and his call to follow him. First, he wanted people to be set free from thinking poorly of themselves in relationship with God. Second, however people imagined God, they were not to fear God. Third, he wanted people to stop being dependent on religious middle management for access to God. They were to discover the presence of God in their everyday living. This presence was not a commodity that people with special religious powers could control, make possible, or deny.

All religious leadership faithful to Jesus should strive to help people recognize this presence in their lives, trust it, and give witness to it. Therein lies the failure of the Christian religion, and Catholicism in particular, to be faithful to the dream of Jesus.

This failure found the Church in a ruinous, defensive position when Western society began to undergo radical social change.

Chapter 4

Preservation at All Costs

The need for the Church to reform itself came to a head in the sixteenth century.

Some of the popes had led scandalous lives. Church appointments, such as those for bishops and cardinals, were sold to the highest bidder. Princes and secular rulers bought these positions for their sons. Many bishops ruled over or "owned" several dioceses as a way of making money through taxes. In many places this meant there was no residing bishop in a diocese, yet alone one who had any concern for pastoral care. Most priests were uneducated. The Mass, especially the elevation of the host after the consecration, had become linked with magic and superstition. The laity were not being nourished with a worthwhile faith vision of life. This was a sick Church becoming worse as the years went by.

What prompted the start of the Reformation?

On the doctrinal level, the central issue was raised by Martin Luther. This grew out of his own personal anxiety about being "saved." How could he, a sinner, know God had really forgiven him? Would he have to make up for his sins by "good works"? In that case, is being "justified" before God something we humans can do for ourselves?

Luther was an Augustinian monk, and his religious superior led him to find solace and the answer to his questions in Paul's letter to the Romans. There, Luther came to belief in God's utter graciousness. He would not be saved by his own efforts, but rather by his trust in God's gracious forgiveness. This was not a new insight in itself, but the focus on faith as more important than the good works we do became a feature of Luther's thought and preaching.

 Why was this so troubling to Church authority?

Luther looked at how the Church gave witness to its faith in God's graciousness and was scandalized by what he saw. In particular he saw the Church dealing in indulgences to raise money. The practice was not new, but Pope Leo X had set up a highly organized campaign in Germany of selling indulgences to fund the restoration of St. Peter's in Rome. This practice of selling "time off" in Purgatory appalled Luther. He preached that the Church, and especially the pope, had no power over God. The pope could not dictate how God was to act in the next life. Luther believed and preached that the practice of selling indulgences insulted God's graciousness. There was no doubt in his mind that the practice was a long way removed from Jesus' teaching or anything in the Scriptures.

Luther had no intention of breaking from the Church, but Church officials did not take kindly to someone attacking the pope along with attacking a source of great revenue. Luther came under several Church investigations, especially for his beliefs concerning papal power, papal primacy, and the infallibility of Church councils. He taught that councils could err. He was very critical of the Council of Constance, which had condemned and burnt John Hus, a Czech priest, one hundred years previously. Hus had stressed the role of Scripture as the source of belief, condemned the sale of indulgences, and preached that only God can forgive sins.

It was basically on his denial of the infallibility of councils that Rome denounced Luther as a heretic and excommunicated him in 1521. This must have seemed a convenient tactic at the time by the Roman authorities. It meant they would not have to take any notice of a heretic's call for reforms. They could trust that Luther's influence and his ideas would fade quite rapidly.

 Why didn't Luther just fade into the background?

Luther was basically a catalyst who enabled widespread, deep-seated unrest in the Church to surface. Just seven years before Luther was born, Girolamo Savonarola, a famous Dominican preacher in Florence, was excommunicated and executed because he had denounced the pope and the papal court. In Luther's time, papal authority, papal corruption, papal control over all aspects of the Church as well as control over land, and the campaign for raising money for Rome were highly unpopular issues in Germany. There was also growing resistance in universities to Church control. Previous councils had failed to bring genuine reform. Luther was able to articulate a way forward for the Church: return to the primacy of Scripture, to the primacy of Jesus, and to the primacy of grace and faith — over papal powers and decrees, over all human achievements and good works, and over magic and superstition. His call for the reform of monasteries, the priesthood, and the sacraments; for more education, to return focus onto Scripture and God's graciousness; and for the Church to remove itself from trying to rule the world and to show greater concern for the poor resonated with many Christians.

It seems that it was not doctrinal differences, as such, that sparked the Reformation?

That is correct. While the topic of "justification" was widely discussed during the Reformation and has been ever since, it was not the cause of the Reformation.

Is this topic still being discussed as a matter of importance for faith?

Yes. And this is quite significant. It means that dialogue between Protestant and Catholic theologians as well as the positions adopted by each side for almost five hundred years have relied on belief in an elsewhere God in heaven.

In effect, then, the Reformation was more about shifting chairs around on a sinking ship rather than repairing the ship?

81

Yes. While there was much-needed change on the level of worship and practice, doctrinal thought stayed immersed in a schema far removed from belief in the universality of God's presence. Everyone thought in terms of the traditional Christian mind-set: original sin, an elsewhere God, and people removed from God's presence.

Some of the early Protestant leaders were even more entrenched in this mind-set than their Catholic counterparts. In defending God's "sovereignty," they emphasized humanity's "total depravity." They articulated belief in God "electing" some people for salvation and not others. They taught that Jesus died only for those chosen, using John's Gospel to "prove" their case: "I lay down my life for my sheep." Jesus did not die for the other sheep.

 Granted that both Catholics and Protestants stayed embedded in the elsewhere God mind-set, what changes took place in the Catholic Church?

The great reforming council was held at Trent, with three sessions, under three popes, in 1551–52, 1555–59, and 1562–63.

The council brought new discipline to Church life. Bishops were ordered to live in and care for their dioceses. Each diocese had to ensure its priests were adequately trained and educated. Celibacy for priests was upheld. Priests had to pray daily from a book of prayers, the Breviary. The abuses with the sale of indulgences were to cease. A Missal that standardized the prayers and rubrics for the Mass was introduced — and remained unaltered for four hundred years. Resulting from the council, an Index of forbidden books was published and was to be kept updated to protect Catholics from ideas contrary to Catholic faith or morality. After the council, the use of a catechism, containing a brief summary of Church teaching in simple question-and-answer form, became a useful means of conveying Church teaching.

 What doctrinal issues did the Council of Trent discuss and teach?

The council, while upholding traditional thinking about original sin, taught that humanity is not totally depraved, and certainly not so depraved as to be incapable of aiding its justification before God through good works. So against Luther's rallying cry of "Faith alone," the council insisted on the link between faith and good works. Against Luther's insistence on "Scripture alone," the council taught that both Scripture and tradition were essential elements in the formation of faith.

Whereas Luther taught that baptism and Eucharist were the only valid sacraments, the council taught that the seven sacraments had been founded by Jesus himself and, as such, were of divine origin. With regard to Eucharist, the council upheld the teaching on transubstantiation, on the "real presence" of Jesus, and on the sacrificial nature of the Mass.

The council clearly acknowledged the supremacy of the pope and the hierarchical nature of the Church.

What impact did the Council of Trent have on Catholic Church life?

We can appreciate the reforms that took place, especially with bishops and clergy, but overall, the Council of Trent cemented Catholic thinking and the Catholic population into unquestioning acceptance of a theological schema that was crippling for the Church's future. That schema placed God's presence and guidance with Church authority, not with the people. It demanded uncritical loyalty to the pope and members of the hierarchy. It brought most of Church life under a tight, authoritarian central control. It demanded absolute control over people's minds. Faith, on a popular level, became associated with acceptance of "what the Church teaches" or "what we learned in the catechism." It was a matter of knowing who to trust had the correct answers — and Church authority left Catholics in no doubt where the correct answers were to be found.

The Church's liturgical life and language for the next four hundred years conditioned Catholics to continue imagining they were "exiles," a long way removed from God and dependent on men with special powers to bring God to them in the sacraments.

Trent continued and fortified the "we-will-look-after-you" model of Church. In this model, Church leaders called on Catholics to trust them because the leaders could tell them what God thinks. Leadership possessed religious truth and could tell people what that truth was. Church leaders since Trent have considered themselves to be the guardians of a "deposit of truths" that can never be changed in any way. They have been conditioned by their theology to view themselves as the dispensers of God's presence and pardon. They have felt no need to listen to the voice of God's Spirit in the people.

Apart from the Council of Trent, were there other significant reforming movements or voices in the sixteenth century?

The Jesuits were founded in Paris by a Spaniard, Ignatius of Loyola, in the 1530s. Their impact in helping reform the Church is inestimable. Well-educated themselves, they educated many of the clergy in turn and helped educate Catholics through opening schools, teaching in universities, and promoting the catechism. They wrote extensively in defense of Church teaching. They gave the Church a solid scholarly foundation in its efforts to combat the influence of Protestantism.

Spain also produced at this time one of the most remarkable women in the history of the Church — Teresa of Avila. After many years as a Carmelite nun, she established a small community of nuns intent on prayer and simple living. They nuns became known as "discalced," meaning "without shoes." Despite opposition from the main Carmelite group, Teresa opened many convents, and the nuns eventually became a separate religious order.

Teresa's other great legacy to reforming the Church was her writing on prayer. Her most famous writing, *The Interior Castle*, is considered a spiritual masterpiece. Like Julian of Norwich, Teresa urged her readers to find the presence of God deep within themselves and to converse with God there.

 What an extraordinary difference we find throughout history. Men fighting over theological concepts and how to control what people think — and women urging people to find God present in the depths of their own being.

Yes, the pattern is there. Throughout history male Church leaders have exhibited the conviction that controlling what people think about doctrine is more important than helping people discover and rejoice in God's intimate presence with them.

 I cannot imagine women instituting the Inquisition. The need to control what Catholics thought and not have them disturbed by Protestant thinking gave rise to the Inquisition, didn't it?

It gave rise to its revival. The Inquisition had its beginning early in the thirteenth century when Pope Innocent III wanted to crush the Albigensian heretics in southern France. The Albigenses, or Cathari as they were otherwise known, were an antisocial sect who believed Satan controlled the material universe. The pope used military force effectively. In one town, Beziers, every man, woman, and child was slaughtered. The papal system of Inquisition, a tribunal system of inquiry to hunt down suspected heretics, originated in this brutal campaign. The pope gave his delegates special powers, making them independent of local bishops, who until then had the responsibility of keeping the local community free from error. In 1233 Gregory IX shaped the process into a formal system of "inquisitors," usually Dominican or Franciscan friars. Victims were often accused anonymously. They were not allowed to call witnesses in their favor. The use of torture, officially approved by Pope Innocent IV in 1252, extracted confessions of guilt from both innocent and guilty parties.

In the fifteenth century, the system of Inquisition was revived in parts of Europe, at the urging of Cardinal Caraffa, to counter the Reformation. Cardinal Caraffa had earlier worked for reconciliation with the Protestants, but finding this impossible, urged strong measures be taken. When he later became pope, he supported the proposition that people who had given up the Catholic faith and would not return should be eradicated before they had a chance to lead other people astray. He said they should be removed like cancer. Once again, the Church did not hesitate to use torture, but stopped short of executions since canon law prevented priests from shedding blood. This was not a problem, though. Anyone deserving the death penalty was handed over to the civil authority to perform the execution.

 The Catholic Church throughout its history seems to have expended a lot of time and energy in controlling the way people think.

Yes, and the Reformation made it even more imperative for Catholic Church authority to adopt strict controls over people's minds. The Church did not want Catholics being disturbed by Protestants quoting Scripture, so the catechism, with its simple question–brief answer format, became the great teaching vehicle of the Counter Reformation period. Nor did the Church want the faith of Catholics to be disturbed by thinking available in the print media. The Index of prohibited books that resulted from the final session of the Council of Trent included almost three-quarters of the books printed in Europe at the time. Trent decreed that any Catholic reading a prohibited book incurred automatic excommunication. The Index was updated regularly in the following centuries (up to the mid-twentieth century) and was used by Church authority as a tool to keep the faithful uninformed about any scientific development or historical knowledge (and later, any Catholic scholarship) that might disturb their faith.

Rome would tell the "simple faithful" what to think and what to believe. The tactic worked wonderfully well. It ensured that at the time of the Second Vatican Council the Catholic laity was generally historically and scripturally ignorant and unable to defend their faith beyond the level of this-is-what-I-was-taught. This, however, was a small price to pay for producing an immense body of laity fiercely loyal to the Catholic institution. Catholics generally did not realize it, but their theological thinking had been very effectively controlled by central Church authority up to the

Second Vatican Council. Until the council, most Catholics throughout the Western world had unquestionably accepted, for example, that the story of Adam's fall from a state of perfect harmony with God related an actual event.

? **It sounds like an authoritarian system of control. It is no wonder the Church resisted the social, scientific, and intellectual developments of the last four centuries.**

The Church's attitude to the secular world in these centuries clearly illustrates the shortcomings of its theological mind-set. A Church in touch with an inclusive understanding of Pentecost and the presence of God's Spirit at work in all places might have been able to rejoice in human progress through social developments, increased scientific knowledge, new ideas, and learning from the past. It might have had a different appreciation of the text in Isaiah,

> Now I am revealing new things to you,
> things hidden and unknown to you,
> created just now, this very moment,
> of these things you have heard nothing until now,
> so that you cannot say, "Oh yes, I knew all this."
>
> (Isa. 48:6–7)

But the Catholic Church, theologically, was unable to do so. Theologically, the Church *had* to resist "new things," to be fearful, and to isolate itself. When the Age of Enlightenment dawned in the seventeenth century, it found Church leadership shrouded in a theological cocoon, unable to adapt to a rapidly changing society. The Church's theologians were not allowed to adapt their thinking to new knowledge and help the Church take account of a worldview radically different from that of the past.

 I presume this is why the Church banned Galileo?

Yes. In the sixteenth century the Polish astronomer Nicholas Copernicus established the revolutionary idea that the earth and other planets circled the sun. Copernicus, knowing the Church would oppose his findings, prudently ensured that his ideas were published after he died and was careful to promote his ideas as hypothesis rather than fact. In 1600, when Galileo was thirty-six, the philosopher-monk Giordano Bruno was burnt at the stake for espousing the Copernican view of the cosmos and for preaching that the universe has a soul. Johannes Kepler and Galileo were convinced that Copernicus was right, and both must have known they were treading on dangerous ground when they promoted his ideas.

The Copernican notion of the cosmos was rejected by the Church on theological grounds. Not only was the earth considered to be the center of God's creation, but since the Book of Joshua records the extraordinary event of the sun "standing still," the Church believed it must be moving around the earth. While Kepler managed to keep clear of conflict with Church authorities, Galileo was more forthright in challenging both the ancient and the medieval concept of the cosmos. Church authorities believed his writings undermined the authority of the Bible and the credibility of Church teaching, so late in life he was ordered to retract, before a Roman Inquisitional panel of cardinals, what he had written. He had to swear that his findings were heretical and contrary to Scripture. He had to pronounce that the sun moves, that the earth is the center of the universe, and that it does not move.

When Galileo died, the pope prohibited a public funeral. Any public observance, stated the pope, would not be fitting for someone who had caused "the greatest scandal in all of Christendom." It would also, he said, be offensive to "the reputation of the Holy Office."

 The Catholic Church did offer a public apology for the way it treated Galileo.

Yes, it did — 350 years after his death. It issued a "Report" admitting Church authorities had acted wrongly. The report mentions "certain theologians who failed to grasp the profound, nonliteral meaning of the Scriptures when they described the physical structure of the created universe. This led them unduly to transpose a question of factual observation into the realm of faith."

Galileo's judges, according to this Report, "incapable of dissociating faith from an age-old cosmology, believed quite wrongly that the adoption of the Copernican revolution, in fact not yet definitively proven, was such as to undermine Catholic tradition, and that it was their duty to forbid it being taught."[3]

The point of being "incapable" is significant. It would be wrong to suggest that Galileo's judges should have known better. In reality they were the products of a theological mind-set that had developed over fifteen hundred years. The significant issue is whether Catholic Church leadership in these times has learned not to associate faith with an "age-old cosmology" and not to insist that faith founded on that old cosmology — such as the Bible's story of creation and an actual "fall" — is certain knowledge.

 I understand the Church was troubled as much by intellectuals in this age as it was by Galileo or other scientists.

This was the Age of Enlightenment. It derives its name from thinkers who considered themselves to be "enlightened" by rational thinking and scientific data and freed from subservience to Church dogma. Rationalism trusted human reason. Empiricism trusted scientific data — what could be proven by the senses to exist. Reason, experience, and scientific data replaced the authority of the Bible and the Church for many intellectuals. Some rationalists saw no need for a God: everything could be explained by natural laws. Some, who reasoned God existed, held that God withdrew and allowed the universe to operate on scientific laws. Most saw no need for a personal God or for Jesus to be the personal revelation of God.

This was indeed a new age, when thinkers applied their minds to all aspects of human life, rejecting the demand of Church authority to stay within its bounds of what constituted certainty. The Church was unable to meet the thinkers on the level of open discussion and examination of objective data. It found itself under attack for holding to dogmas that were "mystery." The rationalists had no regard for religious "mysteries."

 That must have been a no-win situation for the Church, since its statements about God are inevitably about the mysterious — a reality beyond our senses.

While that is true, the reality is that the Church had backed itself into a corner by aligning faith with absolute acceptance of everything in the Bible — as the Galileo affair showed — and was "incapable" of adjusting its faith perspective to new scientific data. Consequently, it lost respect in the academic and the scientific world. The Church discovered, to its horror, in the seventeenth century, that thinking people were no longer willing to give credence to dogma shaped in the worldview of the fourth century and reliant on the biblical account of creation. Sir Isaac Newton, the most outstanding scientist of the seventeenth century, who strongly defended belief in God, maintained that Athanasius led the Church astray in insisting on a scenario that required Jesus to be God in order to save humanity.

The real tragedy seems to be not the alienation of the Church from intellectuals and scientists, but that the Church was not able to rejoice in and help contribute to the sense of wonder that was emerging about God's creation.

93

Yes, the Church had no way of adjusting unless it admitted some of its beliefs were ill-founded and wrong. That was not likely to happen within an institution that considered itself to be the unique medium of God's presence in the world. Nor was it likely to happen in an institution that had wielded unquestioned power and authority for centuries. Inquisitional processes had driven that point home. Unable to appreciate or even to conceptualize an understanding of God's presence at work among people, the Church became defensive, more dogmatic, and isolated from the movements of change within Western society.

 I have often heard from Church officials the statement, "The Church is not a democracy." At one level, I think that's okay, and I can accept it. At another level, though, I think the statement carries a deep-seated resistance to listening to the presence or movement of the Spirit of God in people. I can sense a reactionary, defensive attitude that possibly has its roots in this historical period.

"Democracy" was definitely not one of the Church's favored concepts in the eighteenth and nineteenth centuries. The democratic movement in society brought trouble and shame to the Church and intensified the Church's defensive stance toward the world.

The democratic movement was naturally resisted by the monarchs, who ruled with absolute power, and by the wealthy class. In France the peasants had been living in poverty for centuries. Poverty in towns was rampant. Despite notable exceptions, such as Vincent de Paul, who devoted their lives to working among the poor, the clergy aligned themselves with the rich and the powerful. The clergy were more concerned with keeping favor with the rich. The poor saw the Church aligned with the monarchs in their claim to rule by "divine right."

The French Revolution in 1789 brought together the intellectual movement supporting people's rights to govern themselves and the acute discontent of the populace. In the violent years that ensued, the Church was considered to be the enemy siding with the rich and powerful. Forty thousand priests were driven into exile; twenty thousand of them abandoned the priesthood; many hundreds were slaughtered. Church property was confiscated by the state, and the Church lost its privileges. In this climate there was little hope in the following century that Church leadership would support Catholic thinkers in sympathy with the ideals of the French Revolution and freedom of expression. Liberalism and democracy were seen by Church leadership to be anti-Church and therefore extremely dangerous.

 It seems the Church was off-side with everyone!

Not quite. There was inevitably a reaction from powerful conservative political forces against democratic and liberal ideas. The Church aligned itself with these forces, doubtless concerned for the protection of good order in society, an order it considered to be divinely ordained.

95

It hardly seems a wise thing to do in the circumstances.

We have the luxury of being able to look back knowing the Church was siding with the wrong forces. But at the time the French Revolution seemed to be the work of Satan. It seemed obvious that the fruits of the democratic, liberal movement were evil and had to be resisted.

The issue of wisdom has more to do with whether the Church learned anything from the mistakes it made in aligning itself with conservative political forces fearful of adaptation to significant social changes.

 In that case the Church has acted most unwisely. It not only aligned itself with reactive conservative forces whose style of ruling was coming to an end; it clearly established itself as a major conservative force and continued to rule its followers in the manner of an absolute monarch.

Yes, far from reading the signs of the times from what has happening in society, the Church in the second half of the nineteenth century did everything it could to strengthen its hard-line stance. Some Catholic intellectuals, sensing that the age of rule by monarchy was over in Europe, urged Rome to put faith in people. A French priest, Felicité de Lamennais, widely considered a man of great insight and genius, called on the Church not to fear liberalism, but to "Catholicize" it. He and other thinkers believed that freedom for individuals would be for the good of humanity. He wanted a strong papacy, but one that would support freedom of education, freedom of the press, and a greater separation of Church and state. Condemned by French bishops, he appealed to the pope directly only to find his views denounced in an encyclical, *Mirari Vos,* in 1832. The pope made it clear that any thoughts about freedom of conscience were madness, freedom of the press abhorrent, and distancing the Church from control over states unthinkable.

 It seems the die was cast. Did it get any worse?

Yes, far worse.

In 1846 Pius IX was elected pope.

During his long pontificate major issues faced the Church: the push for intellectual freedom; scientific theories such as those of Charles Darwin; historical research that revealed that important aspects of "tradition" did not go back as far in history as Church authority had maintained; Scripture scholarship that questioned traditional understanding of the date and authorship of biblical texts; the upsurge of democratic processes in politics.

Pius IX was chased out of Rome early in his pontificate because of democratic movements within Italian politics. He was not likely to be sympathetic to democratic causes when he returned in 1850.

Two large gatherings of theologians in 1863 — one in France, the other in Germany — strongly advocated greater freedoms in the Church. In 1864 Pius IX countered with an encyclical, *Quanta Cura,* to which the famous Syllabus of Errors was attached. In the encyclical, Pius IX wrote of the "insane raving" that was "especially injurious to

the Catholic Church" — "namely, that freedom of conscience and of worship is the proper right of each man
and that this should be proclaimed and asserted in every
rightly constituted society." The Syllabus of Errors demonstrated the Church's siege mentality even further. In it
the pope condemned eighty errors. Among them was the
proposition that it was no longer expedient that the Catholic religion should be the only state religion. The pope also
condemned the proposition that the pope ought to reconcile and harmonize himself with progress, liberalism, and
modern civilization. It was unfortunate that the document
did not specify that what the pope meant by "civilization" in this context was "a system invented on purpose
to weaken, and perhaps to overthrow, the Church."[4] The
bald Papal denial that the Church had to reconcile itself
with progress and modern civilization created anger and
confusion everywhere, and the effects were long-lasting.

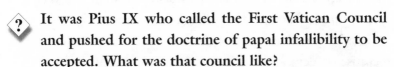

**It was Pius IX who called the First Vatican Council
and pushed for the doctrine of papal infallibility to be
accepted. What was that council like?**

Vatican I (1869–70) starkly revealed the climate of suspicion and mistrust in which Pius IX ruled. He established
the ground rules according to which only he could propose
questions for the council. He disregarded and overturned
the way issues were traditionally decided in Church councils. The Church's tradition had been to work toward moral
unanimity. Pius IX decreed that a simple majority would be
sufficient. This became a key factor in the bitter debate on

papal infallibility and the fact that the topic was discussed at all. The supporters of an extremist statement on infallibility (in chapter 11 of a document on the Church to be discussed) perceived that the council would take a year or so to get to that chapter, so they petitioned the pope to have the topic of papal infallibility discussed first. There was certainly no moral unanimity among the bishops on this, some protesting that it was not fitting to discuss the topic before discussing the Church as a whole.

They would have protested even more strongly had they known the council would never get the chance to discuss other Church issues. The pope had chapter 11 recast as a separate constitution of four chapters on the role of the pope and shifted it to the top of the list for discussion. Debate on the issue lasted from mid-May until July 18, 1870, when the final text of a less extremist statement on papal infallibility was approved by majority vote. The council then went into recess until November, but in September troops for a united Italy took over control of Rome. The pope declared himself a prisoner. The council was never reconvened. The lasting legacy of the First Vatican Council to the future Church desperately struggling with the challenges confronting it was disastrous. It set in progress a Roman attitude of "creeping infallibility" intrinsically linked with a theology of salvation that is elitist. That theology gives men in the corridors of power in Rome the right to control every major aspect of Church life without their authority or their decision-making procedures being questioned.

Was there any reaction from Catholic scholars at the time?

Some Catholic scholars in the first decade of the twentieth century refused to be subdued by Roman condemnations of all ideas that disturbed traditional thought. Their writings precipitated the "modernist" crisis in the Church. Just as "civilization" became a suspect word in Papal circles, so did "modernist," even more so. To be a modernist was to be an enemy of the Church, and the net was thrown over any scholar who proposed "new" ideas that questioned or undermined traditional beliefs and practices. Many of these new ideas arose from historical and scriptural studies. Some of the ideas proposed by the Church's own scholars included:

+ Jesus did not institute seven sacraments.

+ Jesus did not establish the hierarchal structure of the Church or the Roman papacy.

+ Dogmas should not to be seen as unchangeable, but as efforts to makes sense of experience at a particular time in history.

+ There are factual errors in the Bible.

+ Moses did not write the first five books of the Bible.

+ Jesus' knowledge was limited, and he could have made errors of judgment.

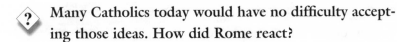 **Many Catholics today would have no difficulty accepting those ideas. How did Rome react?**

In July 1907 the Holy Office issued a decree, *Lamentabili,* condemning sixty-five errors, including those listed above. In September Pope Pius X issued the encyclical *Pascendi,* which severely criticized the philosophical premises of the modernists. However, it went much further. A Church historian notes,

> It presumes bad faith and imputes evil motives to zealous Catholic scholars who were at least asking the right questions, and it presents a sad spectacle of the highest authority in the Church resorting to sarcasm and invective in what was supposed to be a magisterial judgment; it abounds in such harsh phrases as "poisonous doctrines . . . most pernicious of all the adversaries of the Church . . . the root of their folly and error . . . boundless effrontery."[5]

The pope called for strict measures to counteract the influence of modernism.

Every diocese in the Catholic Church was expected to set up vigilance committees to watch for any signs of modernist thinking. The committees were required to operate in secrecy and report directly to Rome. Every diocese had to have censors to screen all writings connected with the Church.

 I have heard people calling some present-day Catholic scholars modernists, and I never knew what they meant.

Throughout the twentieth century "modernist!" became the catch cry of ultra-conservative Catholics afraid of any new ideas in scriptural or theological studies. It was used as an accusation of disloyalty to Church teaching and Church authority. These accusations were frequently made by people lacking any scholarly credentials. Despite this, they would attack, denounce, and report to Rome or to the local bishop scholars who had devoted their lives and scholarship to the Church. The attacks were usually on the basis that the "faith" they had learned so well (that is, the traditional theological schema of salvation) was being undermined by these thinkers.

 I remember taking an oath against modernism before I was ordained in 1963. I cannot remember anything about it though.

Pope Pius X decreed in 1907 that every candidate for priestly ordination had to take an oath against modernism prior to ordination. The decree remained in effect until 1967, when it was replaced by the Profession of Faith, updated in 1989. What is remarkable is that every bishop who attended the Second Vatican Council had sworn this solemn oath against modernism prior to his ordination and in it stated:

> Furthermore, with due reverence, I submit and adhere with my whole heart to the condemnations, declarations, and all the prescripts contained in the encyclical *Pascendi* and in the decree *Lamentabili*.

It makes Vatican II all the more remarkable for what it achieved, but it also explains the diehard resistance to and reaction against the council by conservative factions who saw the council as a victory for modernist thinking and a betrayal of the oath they had pledged.

What is the current situation of the "Profession of Faith"?

The Profession of Faith that became mandatory in 1989 for anyone "assuming an office to be exercised in the name of the Church" is far more than a profession of faith. It concludes with these words as an "oath of fidelity":

> What is more, I adhere with religious submission of will and intellect to the teachings which either the Roman pontiff or the college of bishops enunciate when they exercise the authentic Magisterium even if they proclaim those teachings in an act that is not definitive.

This exercise in mind control is breathtaking. It takes us back centuries to the absolute, unquestioned rule of monarchs.

It may be even worse than that. It takes us back to the Inquisitional system of thought control. There is a subtle threat here: fail to do this and we will remove you from the position you hold. We will see the ruthlessness of that system still operating in Rome when we consider movements in contemporary theology.

Before we move to the present day, though, let us consider Church expansion in the centuries since the Reformation and how theological thought impacted on the missionaries' attitudes toward indigenous people. The underlying issue will be whether the missionaries imagined they were bringing God's presence and "salvation" to people or whether, like Jesus, they urged people to recognize and name the presence of God always with them.

Chapter 5

Preaching in a New World

Pope Alexander VI (1492–1503) will be found in any list of popes notorious for their abuse of the papacy immediately prior to the Reformation. Apart from his corruption he is noteworthy because he divided the world into two and gave one half to Portugal to explore and conquer and the other half to Spain. He then allowed the rulers of both countries to appoint the bishops in the new lands. Inevitably, the greatest expansion of the Church throughout the world involved the missionaries in most places working hand in hand or side by side with the conquering force.

The Aztecs in Mexico and the Incas in the Andes learned with great humiliation that the Spanish conquerors were brutal, deceptive, and intent on stealing the gold and silver that adorned their temples. In Mexico, Hernán Cortés betrayed the trust of the Aztecs and had his men slaughter and loot. In the Andes, Francisco Pizarro engaged in the widespread massacre of the Incas and enslaved many to work in the silver mines. An eyewitness recorded Pizarro telling the conquered leader of the Incas,

We come to conquer this land . . . that all may come to a knowledge of God and of His Holy Catholic Faith; and by reason of our good mission. God, the Creator of heaven and earth and of all things in them, permits this, in order that you may know Him and come out from the bestial and diabolical life that you lead.[6]

These conquerors also brought new diseases with them that within a hundred years reduced the indigenous population by 90 percent.

The missionaries who followed the soldiers into these lands doubtless showed greater compassion and care for the people. But they, too, usually operated with cultural and religious biases that had little appreciation of God's presence in indigenous people or in their religious customs and traditions.

 Was this the way the missionaries worked everywhere?

The Jesuits working in China in the seventeenth century had a different approach. They were helped by the fact that missionaries in China were not allied with a conquering army. The Jesuits, however, differed from other Catholic missionaries in their approach to indigenous people by seeking to adapt to Chinese culture. This sparked a fierce debate in Catholic missionary circles: whether converts from native cultures should make a complete break from their non-Christian culture or whether the missionaries themselves should make an effort to adapt as far as possible to the local culture. Rome was called upon to decide.

In 1622 Pope Gregory XV had established the Sacred Congregation for the Propagation of the Faith in an attempt to bring Catholic missions under Rome's control. This replaced the former system of missionaries working under the umbrella of patronage granted to the Catholic monarchs of Spain and Portugal. The "Propaganda," as it came to be called, soon became a great success in recruiting and training missionaries, in providing financial aid, in supplying catechetical and liturgical aids, and especially in establishing vicar-apostolics in missionary lands. The vicar-apostolics had the full authority of bishops and were seen to be independent of Portuguese and Spanish civil control and the rivalry between religious orders, such as the Jesuits, the Franciscans, and the Dominicans.

In 1659 Propaganda ruled in favor of the Jesuit approach in China. By 1674 the Chinese mission had a Chinese vicar-apostolic. The victory, however, was short-lived, and in 1704 Pope Clement XI banned the Jesuit approach, despite entreaties from the Chinese emperor. Within seven years, almost all missionaries were expelled, and the converts left behind were persecuted. The Jesuit missionary approach in China, built on respect for the presence of God's Spirit in native religions, was in ruins.

 Why did the pope ban the Jesuit approach when it was obviously winning respect among the people and the emperor?

The pope acted under pressure from members of the other religious orders working in China, especially those from Spain. These clergy objected strongly to the Jesuits saying Mass in Chinese, dressing like the Chinese, and tolerating Chinese religious customs.

Their objections resulted from a theological mind-set: God can be present and active only in Westernized, Roman-approved rituals, symbols, and behavior patterns.

The course set by Rome was already standard practice in other countries. It is significant that the Spanish missionaries in California and New Mexico refused to train Native American clergy. The missionaries imposed a "story" of creation that was utterly foreign to Native Americans. The missionaries regarded the native religion as idolatry. They came as the saviors, insisting there was no hope of eternal life with the Creator unless the people embraced their religion. They effectively belittled belief that the Creator Spirit could be present in the native culture and religion.

The missionaries often worked hand in hand with Spanish military, civil, and business forces, which virtually enslaved the people and did not hesitate to use force and murder to keep control.

The Franciscan missionaries had the Native Americans build large churches, a way of impressing the people with the majesty of the new religion. Adjoining the church was a *convento,* rooms for the priests and their servants. This was constructed in a way that allowed the priests to use roof walks to observe the daily activities of the people. There was no mistaking who the "head" of the community was and who had to be obeyed. The "head" of the community could demand that any building, such as an Indian kiva, which could stand as a symbol of traditional belief and practice, could be destroyed.

The kiva is an Indian ceremonial chamber, used to conduct religious ceremonies to ritualize and to bring about harmony between the spirit world and the daily life of the people. It is also used as a place to teach the younger generation the community's cultural values. The many ruins of kivas throughout the countryside are witness to the long-term effects of Catholicism's religious and cultural violence toward Native Americans. They witness to the inevitable breakdown of belief and the enforced practice built on the premise that God's creative and life-giving presence can only be present when a superior force dominates and destroys a culture that for many centuries gave people bonding, meaning, and a sense of connectedness with the Unknown Mystery.

 Have we learned from the mistakes made?

There is no doubt that Catholic missionaries throughout the world work today with a quite different, highly respectful approach to indigenous people and their traditional religious beliefs and practices. However, some of the ruinous elements of the theological thinking that motivated earlier missionary work still remain in official Catholic Church teaching. Church leadership in Rome today still insists on unquestioning acceptance of its theological schema on salvation. Church leadership still wants to impose everywhere a story about creation and God's activity in it that no longer has credibility. This story is not the Western world's story of meaning and connectedness anymore, just as it was never the story of meaning and connectedness for the Chinese or the Australian aboriginal people or the Native Americans.

Church leadership, in proclaiming the Church as the sacrament of the encounter with God, still fails to recognize with any semblance of respectability God's presence and activity in other religions. The Church officially declared in 2000 that only its sacred writings are "inspired" by God. It still officially proclaims that God wants everyone to be part of "His" Church. Rome still seeks to control liturgical practice and language according to Western images and ideas.

Rome's contemporary theological position continues institutional religion's tragic mistake of separating people from connectedness with God in order to bolster claims for the particular religion's founder or the religion's uniqueness. Rather than starting with the premise that everyone is born intimately connected with God and then articulating how the life, message, death, and resurrection of Jesus validate this premise, Rome's theology starts with separation from God and presents Jesus as the only possible means of access to God.

Chapter 6

Doctrine and Church Renewal

 I read recently that doctrine is essential for the life of the Church, that it gives identity to what the Church is and who we are as members of the Church. The writer said this is why doctrine cannot change. What do you think?

Doctrine is important in giving identity to the Church as an institution and to ourselves as members of the Church. However, doctrine can also grant absolute power and authority to a select few, as it has in the Catholic Church. This may be why Jesus had no interest in doctrine. It would be fair to assume that Jesus would be greatly disturbed by any doctrine granting absolute power and authority to religious leaders at the expense of respecting God's presence in all people. He would be disturbed by the use of force and the threats of punishment to impose uniform doctrinal belief. He would be disturbed by doctrine based on belief that every baby is born into a state of separation from God. He would be disturbed by doctrinal notions that only he could gain access to God for humankind.

? **You are suggesting that doctrine *should* change?**
Definitely.

? **But the Church says its doctrine can never change!**
Let us imagine some changes.

Let us imagine the Church as the institutional bearer of the good news that God is present in every human person. Let us imagine that the Church were to preach this consistently and were to respect this presence even in religions quite different from itself. Let us imagine that the Church through its sacramental life constantly sought to affirm this presence in its members and encouraged them to give bold witness to it. Let us imagine the Church as a powerful voice in our world calling for respect and justice based on all of humankind's union with the one God, whatever the cultural and religious differences. Let us imagine the Church calling its members to gather around the story of Jesus because his life and preaching reveal to us the wonder of who we are.

What would change? Several things, none of them presently acceptable to Rome.

One. The Church would have to stop proclaiming belief in a God who requires Jesus to suffer and die in order to heal the "rupture" caused by Adam's sin. This extremely primitive notion of God has no credibility outside the Church. It cannot continue as the ground of communication with today's world about humankind's relationship with God.

Is this belief about Jesus having to suffer and die because of Adam's sin still central to Catholic doctrine?

It is not at all prominent in the thinking of many Catholic theologians. However, this theology of salvation is not only prominent, it has pride of place, in the teaching of Pope John Paul II and Cardinal Joseph Ratzinger (now Pope Benedict XVI) when he was head of the Congregation for the Doctrine of the Faith (CDF).

Consider these examples of the thinking of the Magisterium of the Catholic Church as Catholics embraced the twenty-first century.

The Congregation for the Doctrine of the Faith in August 2000 in its declaration *Dominus Iesus* informed bishops and theologians what "must be believed and taught":

> As an innocent lamb he merited life for us by his blood which he freely shed. In him God reconciled us to himself and to one another, freeing us from the bondage of the devil and of sin.[7]

Pope John Paul II, in his *Exhortation to the Church in Europe* after the synod of European bishops, wrote:

> He is the Lamb standing before the throne of God (cf. Rev. 5:6): sacrificed, because he shed his blood for us on the wood of the Cross.[8]

The *Catechism of the Catholic Church* states:

113

> The Father handed his Son over to sinners in order to reconcile us with himself.[9]

Such comments lead to the second item requiring change if the Church is to have a relevant voice in the world: the notion of the elsewhere God that permeates this thinking. Church leadership would have to scrutinize doctrine and teaching reliant on belief in God as an elsewhere reality and make changes to accommodate a focus on God as an everywhere reality.

A third item is the teaching that Jesus is the only possible savior. The Church would have to respect that God's presence in other cultures and religions is not the result of anything Jesus did. God's presence is and always has been there, active and coming to expression in what is there. The Church would have to acknowledge officially that "salvation" is not primarily about who gets into heaven or not but is more about helping people, as Jesus did, to become more aware of the divine presence within them.

Catholic Church leadership, however, is far removed from acknowledging God's universal presence. Instead of respecting God's presence in diversity, Pope John Paul II, disturbed by "the ethical and religious pluralism which increasingly characterizes Europe," insisted on the need

> to profess and proclaim the truth of Christ as the one Mediator between God and men and the one Savior of the world.[10]

Only Jesus, stated the pope, "grants eternal life."[11]

The declaration *Dominus Iesus* insists that Jesus as the only Savior "must be firmly believed as a constant element of the Church's faith."

With this doctrinal position posited as a line no Catholic bishop or theologian may cross, the declaration then asserts the Church's position:

+ Theology may explore how other religions fall within this "divine plan of salvation."

+ "The Lord Jesus, the only Savior" constituted the Church to continue his work of salvation. "Therefore, the fullness of Christ's salvific mystery belongs also to the Church."

+ "The Church is the universal sacrament of salvation.... She has in God's plan an indispensable relationship with the salvation of every human being."

+ "It is clear that it would be contrary to the faith to consider the Church as one way of salvation alongside those constituted by the other religions."

+ "With the coming of the Savior Jesus Christ, God has willed that the Church founded by him be the instrument for the salvation of all humanity."

+ "If it is true that the followers of other religions can receive divine grace, it is also certain that objectively speaking they are in a gravely deficient situation in comparison with those who, in the Church, have the fullness of the means of salvation."[12]

This seems to be doctrine at the service of the Church seeking unique identity and power rather than doctrine keeping alive the mind and inclusive attitude of Jesus.

And that is why institutional Church leadership will not countenance any questioning of this theology: it grants power and control. It establishes the pope and the Congregation for the Doctrine of the Faith as protectors of the "sacred deposit" and as guardians of the Church's elitist place among all religions. In this theology the Church becomes "the sacrament of God's presence in the world." This being the case, men exercising the highest authority in the Church see themselves as spokesmen for God in the world, as the divinely inspired interpreters of what God "thinks" on any issue.

 So any genuine reform movement in the Church has to deal with doctrine?

Yes, the Reformation and the Counter Reformation failed to help the Church communicate with the world around it because all factions remained in the traditional elsewhere-God doctrinal framework. Vatican I did not even pretend to reform the Church, but set the Church up to fight against the modernists. Vatican II, which gave Catholics so much hope, eventually failed to realize that hope because the Roman doctrinal mind-set exercised absolute control over all aspects of Catholic thought and practice. Until that mind-set is challenged, found wanting, and gives way to a more universal and inclusive understanding of God, Rome will continue to use its power and authority to control, silence, deny, and avoid anything it wants to control, silence, deny, and avoid facing.

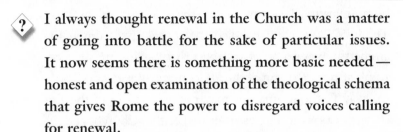

I always thought renewal in the Church was a matter of going into battle for the sake of particular issues. It now seems there is something more basic needed — honest and open examination of the theological schema that gives Rome the power to disregard voices calling for renewal.

Yes, until this is done Roman authority will continue to act as if it is the voice of God in the world, and it will keep demanding unquestioning obedience from bishops, clergy, and laity. Rome will always win. That is the prospect for the future unless and until Catholics concerned for change in the Church bring the questioning of the theological foundation out in the open. The future of the Church depends on it. The crucial task facing the Catholic Church is not the preservation of a past doctrinal worldview but bringing the freeing, inclusive message of Jesus and Pentecost to today's world. That means it must adapt its message to the imagery and language of today.

If I understand this right, the task of renewal is not only that of bringing data about a particular issue to bear — because Rome will just ignore the data if it wants to — but of exposing the theological mind-set that permits Roman and other Church leaders to ignore the voices of renewal?

That's correct. Think of the way leadership in the Church handled the issue of contraception. Think of how it handles the issues of celibacy, divorce and remarriage, homosexuality, women priests, the selection of bishops. Think of how it mishandled the sexual abuse crisis. Examine the way some of our best theologians are silenced. Look at how Roman authority constantly legislates about the way Catholics may or may not participate in the Eucharist. Look at the clericalism of the Church and its patriarchal attitudes toward women. Think of bishops wanting to use Communion as a political weapon.

 That is quite an agenda. Where do we start?

Let us start with how and why Rome silences respectable theologians whose writings could possibly lead us into new faith perspectives.

Chapter 7

Repression of Thought

In 1968 more than thirteen hundred Catholic theologians around the world signed a call for more freedom in theological research in order to stimulate faith in accord with contemporary science and worldview. Eleven years later the Congregation for the Doctrine of the Faith made it clear that the call had been rejected when it investigated the bestselling book *Jesus — An Experiment in Christology* by Edward Schillebeeckx. Schillebeeckx acknowledged in an interview that Roman theologians would not understand his approach to Jesus:

> I tried to help people grasp how Jesus was experienced by his contemporaries. Jesus shows us what God will be for us and also what we must be for God. I do not deny that Jesus is God, but want to assert that he is also man, something that has been overlooked. It is precisely as man that he is important for us. But when you say that, you are suspect. They [Roman theologians] always want you to go on repeating the Chalcedonian formulas.[13]

What disturbed many theologians was not just the fact that the Congregation investigated a highly respected theologian, but the manner in which it did so. Schillebeeckx was never told who made official complaints about his book. He did not know who conducted the first stage of the inquiry or what their theological competence was. When he was finally summoned to Rome he was not told in advance the names of the three men on the investigating panel. He found to his dismay that one of them was Fr. Jean Galot, S.J., who had already publicly linked him with "theologians teaching contrary to the Church." He expected that one of the three panel members would be speaking in his defense, but this was not so.

 Were any voices raised in objection to this process of investigation?

On December 3, 1979, the *Times* of London published a letter signed by eighty-three English theologians protesting the Congregation's methods:

> We believe that measures such as those currently being employed by the Congregation are inconsistent with fundamental human rights, gravely threaten that freedom of interpretation and research which is an indispensable feature of the human quest for meaning and truth, discredit the authority which employs such measures, and imperil that fragile climate of mutual trust between the churches which has developed in recent decades.[14]

Did the Congregation take any notice of the objections?

No. The Congregation has been consistent in its refusal to allow any "freedom of interpretation and research" that permits theologians to query its narrow theology of salvation. The Schillebeeckx case illustrates how the Congregation expects all theologians to remain within the limits of that theology.

The key questions put to Schillebeeckx by the investigating panel focused on:

- "the sacrificial value of the death of Jesus"
- Jesus' awareness that he was the Messiah and the Son of God
- Jesus as founder of the Church
- the virginal conception of Jesus
- the bodily nature of the resurrection
- the institution of the Eucharist by Jesus

Why were those topics chosen?

If we move forward to October 6, 2001, we find Cardinal Ratzinger, then head of the Congregation for the Doctrine of the Faith, giving the answer to that question when he addressed the world Synod of Bishops in Rome:

The central problem of our day seems to me to be the emptying of the figure of Jesus Christ. It begins with the denial of the virginal conception of Jesus in the womb of Mary. It continues with the denial of the bodily resurrection of Jesus, leaving his body to corrupt and transforming the resurrection into a purely spiritual event, leaving no hope for the body, for the material. It continues with the denial of the self-understanding of the Jesus of history as the Son of God, conceding to him as authentic only those words considered possible on the lips of a rabbi of his time. In this way the institution of the eucharist is also cast as impossible for the historical Christ. . . . A Jesus thus impoverished cannot be the one savior and mediator. . . . We must return with clarity to the Jesus of the Gospels, since he alone is also the true historical Jesus: you alone have the words of eternal life. (John 6:68)[15]

So the concern is to protect belief in Jesus as the only savior of the world and thereby protect the Church's position as God's medium of salvation for all people?

Yes, with the understanding that salvation is primarily about how we get into heaven when we die.

I cannot see that my Catholic faith will fall apart if I refuse to believe that Jesus' body physically ascended above the earth somewhere. It seems to me that what Schillebeeckx was examined on and what Ratzinger regards as the "emptying out of Jesus" belongs to healthy theological debate in the Church.

While that may be so, the Congregation for the Doctrine of the Faith insists that Catholics cannot and must not openly debate these issues because its preferred theology of salvation would have to undergo a dramatic change if thinking about these issues were to change. Rome's solution is to ban any honest and open discussion on these issues by declaring them inviolable. This reflects the disingenuous approach of the CDF. Despite its claim to defend and promote "truth," it bans any scholarly voice and ignores any data not in agreement with its favored theology of salvation.

 I find it incomprehensible that as a Catholic I am not supposed to question the teachings on the virgin conception or the "virgin birth" when I know many of my Catholic friends no longer believe them literally and, more importantly, that my faith is not diminished by not believing them anymore. They are not an essential part of the structure of my Catholic faith.

You have plenty of company. The literalness of the virgin conception of Jesus is no longer accepted unquestioningly in mainstream Catholic theology. As far back as 1966 the Dutch bishops resisted Rome's insistence that the virgin conception as a literal fact be included in their catechism. They compromised by allowing an appendix to record the Vatican's teaching. Raymond Brown in his book *The Birth of the Messiah* devoted an appendix to the question of the virginal conception of Jesus and concluded "that the scientifically controllable biblical evidence leaves the question of the historicity of the virginal conception unresolved. The resurvey of the evidence necessitated by the commentary leaves me even more convinced of that."[16]

This statement of Brown highlights the need to keep in mind the distinction between *belief* and *factual data*. Christian tradition considered the evidence available to it, considered that evidence in a theological framework, and made a judgment that Jesus was virginally conceived. Cardinal Ratzinger, now Pope Benedict XVI, upholds that belief. But what he and others who believe in the virgin conception of Jesus do not have the right to do is to elevate the virgin conception to the status of indisputable fact when the research of Church scholars indicates the historicity of the event is "unresolved."

 I think along the same lines with belief about Jesus' resurrection and ascension being physical.

The issue of a bodily, physical resurrection for Jesus is debatable as much as the virgin conception of Jesus. Again, there is no factual proof, and it is significant that St. Paul never refers to it. A belief that death was not the end of Jesus in no way depends on a bodily resurrection, just as a belief that our death will not be the end of us does not depend on a physical resurrection of our bodies. And while biblical stories suggesting Jesus was able to eat and to be touched and then ascended "into heaven" after his death would have caused no problems for the believers who first heard these stories, many twenty-first-century Catholics bring to them an understanding of the universe that makes literal belief impossible. They are not willing to give submission of intellect and will to belief in a human body disappearing into the clouds and then hurtling, one presumes, through space in a journey to "heaven." Traveling at the speed of light the body would still be somewhere on the outer reaches of the Milky Way Galaxy — unless, of course, an interventionist God bypassed the laws of physics and took this physical body somewhere, where this God really lives. Pope Benedict XVI demands that Catholic theologians not engage these awkward points that any educated Catholic might raise, but give public submission of intellect to literal belief in a bodily resurrection. In so doing he demeans Catholic scholars who know they cannot afford to share their scholarly and contrary conclusions with the rest of the Church.

In "The Relationship between Magisterium and Exegetes," a speech given on the hundredth anniversary of the Pontifical Biblical Commission, before he became pope, Cardinal Ratzinger revealed his reliance on an interventionist God and his belief that our faith in this God is to be trusted over and against any scholarship advising against a literal interpretation of certain events in the Gospels.

A God who cannot *intervene* in history and reveal Himself in it is not the God of the Bible. In this way the reality of the birth of Jesus by the Virgin Mary, the effective institution of the Eucharist by Jesus at the Last Supper, his bodily resurrection from the dead — this is the meaning of the empty tomb — are elements of the faith as such, which it can and must defend against an only presumably superior historical knowledge.

That Jesus — in all that is essential — was effectively who the Gospels reveal him to be to us is not mere historical conjecture, but a fact of faith.

? Is this to be understood as the Church's official final word on the subject? Is that how it works? The Congregation rules that the Bible's interventionist God has acted in this way simply because it is in the Gospels — and no one can ask questions?

Cardinal Ratzinger obviously believed it to be the final word. He also knew he had the power to ensure that any theologian teaching in a Catholic institution who publicly contradicted him would lose his teaching position.

? And now he is pope and brings this theological mindset, based on an interventionist God, to ruling the Church!

Yes, even his election to the papacy was conducted in the belief that an elsewhere God had made His decision who the next pope was to be, and the role of the cardinals was to gather in prayer so they could discern whom God had chosen. Cardinal Enio Antonelli, archbishop of Florence, preaching in the Church of San Andrea just prior to the conclave, asserted,

> The new pope has already been chosen by the Lord. We just have to pray to understand who he is.

? It creates an air of certainty, doesn't it, when you oper-ate within these parameters? The elsewhere God, who knows everything and has everything in control, has a plan, and makes a decision. The pope is chosen by God Himself. This circle keeps going round, doesn't it — the theological basis for power and authority?

Yes. Cardinal Ratzinger put fences around the theol-ogy that gave him the right to disregard contrary scholarly opinion. He is not likely to change his position now.

? I grew up thinking Jesus knew everything, including the fact he was God. I think it was in the 1970s that I first came across writing suggesting he was in fact more human than I ever imagined. That has helped deepen my companionship with him rather than weaken it.

It is significant that the Congregation for the Doctrine of the Faith insists theologians must believe and teach that Jesus *knew* he was God. It is significant because it is clear in the early Gospels that Jesus never gave any indication he thought so and never drew attention in any way to himself as "God incarnate." Any reference to Jesus as "son of God" in the context of his public ministry has to be understood in the way the title was generally used at the time: to de-scribe someone in and through whom God did wonderful deeds.

There is a dramatic difference in John's Gospel. The au-thor of this Gospel has Jesus drawing attention to himself as the indispensable way *to* God. Christian tradition has always relied on this theology (developed in John's Gospel well after Jesus' death) to "prove" that Jesus knew he was God incarnate. Today mainstream Catholic Scripture scholarship generally accepts that Jesus spoke few of the words attributed to him in John's Gospel. This posed a major problem for Cardinal Ratzinger and the Congregation for the Doctrine of the Faith. Cardinal Ratzinger acknowledged the problem in a speech, "Current Doctrinal Relevance of the *Catechism of the Catholic Church*," presented on the tenth anniversary of the *Catechism*'s publication:

> Particularly strong attacks were directed against the use of Scripture in the *Catechism:* as previously noted, (it was said) that this work did not take into account a whole century of exegetical work; for example, how could it be so naive as to use passages from the Gospel of John to speak of the historical figure of Jesus; it would be shaped by a literalistic faith which could be called fundamentalist, etc.

Note the "particularly strong attacks." These were criticisms from the Church's own Scripture scholars who declared it was dishonest to quote certain passages from John's Gospel as the actual words of Jesus when there is a wealth of respectable Catholic scholarship acknowledging Jesus never said these words. Cardinal Ratzinger's response in the speech was to dismiss this scholarship as merely "hypothesis" and to assert that "we must keep in mind how rapidly exegetical hypotheses change and, to be honest, how great is the dissent, even among scholars, regarding many theses."

 This sounds like the Galileo affair all over again: Church authority rejects the evidence of its own Church scholars because that evidence conflicts with their theological outlook.

The difference is that we might excuse Galileo's judges because they did not know better. This, on the other hand, is a deliberate choice to reject sound scholarship.

What it means in effect for today's Church is that the pope and the Congregation for the Doctrine of the Faith will determine, in the light of their salvation theology, what events in the Gospels must be accepted as "certain knowledge" — because those "events" make Jesus the "only possible savior."

Cardinal Ratzinger concluded his speech to the synod of bishops with the words: "Let us pray that the Lord will help us be good merchants, faithful administrators of the goods with which we have been entrusted."

It was a significant prayer granted the cardinal's then-pivotal role in the Church and the audience of bishops he was addressing. It is even more significant now that he is the pope. He could have prayed that the Church would have the courage and the openness to bring Jesus' healing and freeing message about the presence of God in our midst to today's world using images and words relevant to these times. Instead, he prayed that the bishops be faithful "administrators of the goods."

Church authority so defensive, so protective of the "goods," so visibly afraid of the Church's scholars and of open discussion is not a sign of hope for the Church's future.

? This reminds me of Carl Sagan, the eminent twentieth-century astronomer, and his lack of confidence in organized religion. He contrasted the demand of the scientific world for rigorous, open examination of data and theory with organized religion's demand that authoritative statements be accepted unquestioningly without any rigorous or open discussion about its findings.

Yes, any religion that refuses to allow its adherents to openly discuss and scrutinize data on which its authoritative teachings depend is inevitably driven by fear — fear that people will discover how illogical or out of touch with reality some of those teachings are.

? The classic case for me was the forced resignation of the Jesuit priest Thomas Reese as the editor of *America* magazine in May 2005. I recall the editor of the *National Catholic Reporter* writing that if the Vatican felt it had to have Reese removed "then this church is in far worse shape than many of us imagined."

Tom Roberts, in his May 19, 2005, editorial of the *National Catholic Reporter,* lauded Reese for being "even-tempered and even-handed in his journalistic treatment of themes" and for "advancing important discussions and honest debate within the church." Roberts's words reflected the high regard in which Reese was held in Catholic journalistic circles. The Congregation for the Doctrine of the Faith, however, pressured the Jesuits to have Reese removed. The Congregation said it was acting in response to complaints from some unnamed U.S. bishops.

 I find it hard to believe my Church operates this way. We had no idea how many, or rather, how few bishops were involved. We had no idea of who they were. We were not told what the specific complaints were. Yet a man who devoted his life to open and fair debate in the Church, a man many of us respected for his integrity, a man who touched our lives through his work, was forced to resign. It seems institutional Church leadership cannot tolerate the laity being informed by articles that bring Church teaching to reflection, scrutiny, and discussion.

Do you hear the echoes here? "It seems institutional Church leadership cannot tolerate the laity being informed"

- about finances
- about deviant sexual behavior of some members of the clergy and the hierarchy
- about the processes for selecting bishops
- about scriptural scholarship
- about history
- about Roman control over bishops' conferences

It is sad and tragic to see institutional Church leadership professing that "the truth will set you free" so fearful of objective data, of scholarship, of open enquiry and discussion, and of a Catholic press bringing that data, scholarship, and discussion to its readers.

Tom Roberts commented in his *NCR* editorial about the Reese resignation, "This was not an act to defend truth, for truth was never in danger in the pages of *America*. This was an act fearful that the truth cannot withstand the challenges that come its way. It's a debilitating fear for a church to exhibit."

This fear and the repression of thought that accompanies it have strengthened once again in the Catholic Church an atmosphere of intellectual dishonesty. Scholars and writers know they cannot afford to share with the body of the Church what they know and think if their knowledge and their thoughts are outside the boundaries of what Rome dictates to be truth beyond question. Rome and Church authority declare they are simply preserving "truth," the "goods." More and more Catholics now know otherwise. They recognize intellectual dishonesty when they see and experience it. Unfortunately, they feel powerless to do anything about it, such is the system of authority operating in the Church.

Chapter 8

Hypocrisy in Religious Dialogue

On the surface, the Catholic Church has made considerable advances in dialoguing with other major religions since the Second Vatican Council, and Pope John Paul II received praise for some of his initiatives. However, at a time in history when genuine dialogue between the major religions seems more crucial than ever for the sake of peace within and among nations, much of what poses as "dialogue" from the Vatican is a facade cloaking beliefs enshrined in a theological schema that ruins any hope of genuine progress.

In 1997 Fr. Jacques Dupuis, S.J., published *Toward a Christian Theology of Religious Pluralism.*[17] Fr. Dupuis was not a liberal theologian. He was seventy-seven years old when he was investigated by the CDF. He had taught theology in India for twenty-five years and in his seventies enjoyed the respect and authority of being professor emeritus at Rome's Gregorian University. He wrote the book expressing his desire to remain faithful to Church doctrine.

The book was generally considered to be a middle-of-the-road exposition of Christian theology suitable for use in dialogue with other religions. The CDF, however, found, as recorded in a Notification confirmed by Pope John Paul II in January 2001,

> notable ambiguities and difficulties on important doctrinal points, which could lead a reader to erroneous or harmful opinions. These points concerned the interpretation of the sole and universal salvific mediation of Christ, the unicity and completeness of Christ's revelation, the universal salvific action of the Holy Spirit, the orientation of all people to the Church, and the value and significance of the salvific function of other religions.

The CDF insisted:

> It must be firmly believed that Jesus is the sole and universal mediator of salvation for all humanity.
>
> It must be firmly believed Jesus Christ is the mediator, the fulfilment and the completeness of revelation. It is therefore contrary to the Catholic faith to maintain that revelation in Jesus Christ (or the revelation of Jesus Christ) is limited, incomplete or imperfect.
>
> It must be firmly believed ... the historical revelation of Jesus Christ offers everything necessary for man's salvation and has no need of completion by other religions.

It must be firmly believed that the elements of truth and goodness found in other religions derive ultimately from the "source mediation of Jesus Christ."

It must be firmly believed that the Church is sign and instrument of salvation for all people. It is contrary to the Catholic faith to consider the different religions of the world as ways of salvation complementary to the Church.

It must be firmly believed that the followers of other religions are oriented to the Church and are all called to become part of her.

It must be firmly believed that whatever the Spirit brings about in human hearts and in the history of peoples, in cultures and religions, serves as a preparation for the Gospel.

 I can recognize much of this as the Catholic faith of my youth, but that was years and years ago. I thought Vatican II had moved the Church well beyond believing that everyone in the world is "called" to be part of the Church.

It is a good example of men so enshrouded in their theological world that they speak the language of elitism and arrogance rather than the language of connectedness and respect. The ramifications of this thinking are enormous for discussion and dialogue both inside and outside the Church.

Inside the Church, leadership continues the long history of repression of thought and forces the Church's theologians, especially those talking and writing about Jesus' role in "salvation," to work publicly in theological straitjackets. In 2005 the CDF repeated much of the above Notification in condemning Fr. Roger Haight's book *Jesus: Symbol of God*. The Notification condemned Haight for casting doubt on the proposition that "Jesus accepted to suffer punishment for our sins or to die to satisfy the justice of God." Imagine! Every Catholic theologian the world over can be reported to Rome and lose his or her teaching position if he or she casts doubt on that proposition! And any theologian daring to suggest publicly that one religion "can no longer insist on being the center to which all the others have to be brought back" had better heed the Notification's warning that this "contradicts the church's traditional faith in Christ as the lone and universal savior of humanity."

Rome expects the bishops of Asia, for example, to make it clear to the leaders of other religions in the region that their religions possess goodness only through the mediation of Jesus, that their religions are but a "preparation" for Christianity, and that all the members of their religions are called to be part of the Catholic Church.

Do the bishops of Asia have any comment on this theology?

The Asian bishops in their 1998 synod had explicitly warned Rome that this type of exclusive, elitist language was damaging to the Church's work in Asia. In response to them, Pope John Paul in his *Exhortation to the Church in Asia* stated that it is the "Father's eternal design" and "desire" that the whole human race may become part of the Church. The Church exists as the "visible plan" of God's love for humanity. The Church alone is "the sacrament of salvation." The Church is "the privileged place of encounter between God and man, in which God chooses to reveal the mystery of his inner life and carry out his plan of salvation for the world." The Church is "the sacrament of the unity of all mankind."[18]

Pope John Paul II also believed and taught

> that the communion of the particular Churches with the Church of Rome, and of their Bishops with the Bishop of Rome, is — in God's plan — an essential requisite of full and visible communion.[19]

 I was never aware of how much that idea of the God who has a "plan" influences Catholic teaching. Did the pope really believe God is a deity in heaven who plots and plans?

We can only answer that by examining what he said and wrote about God. There is evidence enough to suggest that he thought in terms of an elsewhere deity with a "plan" or "design" in mind. Presumably this God looks down or over us with concern that "His" plan is going well. Presumably this God thinks that Catholicism is the only worthwhile religion and wants everyone in the world to see the light soon.

This is hardly a concept or understanding of God that is likely to win friends or influence people in other religions.

And that is one of the greatest disappointments in our world today. This outdated understanding of God is no way suitable for or capable of achieving advancement in religious dialogue. It is an understanding of God that keeps alive religious fundamentalism, advocates religious elitism, and worst of all creates divisions and barriers rather than working toward unity. The world desperately needs religious conversation that will bring people of different religions to a position of mutual respect.

The Catholic Church in its official statements insists on a theology that deepens the wounds of division. The world is in desperate need of a religious message that binds all people in respect for one another. The obvious starting points for Christians are the concepts of God's universal presence and God's "Spirit" at work everywhere in creation. The Catholic Church instead focuses on a concept of God that is narrow, limited, and divisive. The God of *Dominus Iesus* is not a majestic, awesome presence in all of creation. It is the God of the Catholic Church. It is an idol created and worshiped because it gives prestige, power, and authority to men who run the Church. It is a God constructed by human thinking to strengthen elitist, institutional identity.

This isn't the understanding of God that Jesus preached. He urged people to discover the presence of God all around them. Jesus' attitude was: I have something; you

138

have it too. Look at the way you love and care for one another. If you see the sacred in me in the way I live, then learn to recognize the same sacred presence in you. Institutional Church leadership, however, is so concerned with its own elite status in the world and so fearful of "religious pluralism" (a particularly strong fear of the present pope) that it fails to be the sign or manifestation of God's presence in the world the way Jesus was. Why else is this leadership not genuinely interested in helping *all* human beings to be more aware of their innate connectedness with God's presence in their everyday loving? Why else is this leadership unwilling to make this broad, inclusive, truly "catholic" appreciation of God's presence everywhere the starting point for genuine dialogue with other religions? And why else is Church leadership unwilling to accept that the divine presence is beyond the confines of the Christian story and Christian theology and resisting honest exploration of how this acceptance might help the dialogue it professes to want with other religions?

Pope Benedict XVI and the CDF will continue to be extremely wary of "religious pluralism," fearful of "relativism" and Catholics losing appreciation that the Catholic Church is God's own Church.

Rome's failure to be truly expansive and catholic in its understanding of God's universal presence is scandalous both inside and outside the Church. It is scandalous in the way theologians are obliged to adapt their thinking to fit into the narrow limits allowed by the pope and the CDF or risk losing their teaching positions.

Much progress has been made, though, in ecumenical dialogue and respect shown for other religions.

No one could deny there has been progress. However, when the Vatican so clearly articulates its belief that Catholicism is in God's plan the only genuine religion, there comes a point when dialogue becomes window dressing. A clear example of this was the extraordinary phenomenon of Pope John Paul II being directed by his Vatican minders not to pray with leaders of other religions at Assisi in 2002 for fear it might give some credibility to other religions.

The 2002 gathering in Assisi was the second gathering of religious leaders at the invitation of the pope. The first gathering was in October 1986, when the pope in his welcome address to the delegates clarified it was not a meeting to discuss theological issues. The gathering was to express its concern for world peace and to demonstrate that the great religions of the world could rise above their differences and be united in their concern, through shared prayer, for peace in the world. The gathering was a wonderful sign to the world, but, as William Johnson reported in the *Tablet,* not everyone was impressed:

> Some cardinals and theologians of the Roman Curia were less than happy. They could not reconcile Assisi with the teaching of the Catholic Church as set forth in the Catechism of the Council of Trent and the standard work of Heinrich Denzinger. They were educated to believe that worship with non-Catholics (*communicatio in sacris*) was an abomination. The

council, it is true, had permitted and even encouraged prayer with other Christians. But prayer with pagans? No doubt Christians and non-Christians could pray "in the same place." But could they pray "together"? Perish the thought![20]

The events of September 11, 2001, highlighted an even greater need and demand for religious leaders to be united in prayer. Johnson reported that in January 2002, at the pope's invitation, two hundred delegates from twelve of the world's religions met at Assisi to commit themselves to "eliminate the root causes of terrorism" and to proclaim that "violence and terrorism are incompatible with the authentic spirit of religion." This time, reported Johnson,

> ... the preparation was entrusted to the Roman Curia, which made it clear that the religious leaders would not "pray together" but would pray "in different places in the same town." One curial theologian explained that prayer is based on what we believe; and since we believe different things we cannot pray together. The sick and ageing Pope, who had previously said that the challenge of peace transcends religions, now said that there would be no religious syncretism: each group would pray in a different place.

But even these concessions did not satisfy the critics. Some conservative Italian Catholics issued a statement saying that the supreme pontiff was creating confusion among Catholic believers by appearing alongside heretics and unbelievers. More disturbing is the fact that only a handful of cardinals from the Roman Curia agreed to attend the peace meeting.

The present pope sided with the curial officials in their opposition to Pope John Paul II praying with non-Christian religious leaders in Assisi on the grounds that praying with them would diminish Catholicism's distinctiveness. However, in 2006, in a statement acknowledging the twentieth anniversary of the 1986 gathering, he referred to the event as "prophetic" in its appeal to religions to disassociate themselves from war and violence.

 Yes, but this statement carried the usual cautions about religious relativism. The bottom line still seems to be that only the Catholic Church has the fullness of truth, and we have to be very careful about engagement with other religions in case we give ground or lose our unique identity as the only "true" religion. Is there any hope for significant change of thinking?

As with some other significant issues the change of thinking will inevitably come from the ground up, not from the top down since leadership at the top is clearly preoccupied with protecting institutional identity and uniqueness. The hope lies in our willingness to be involved in inter-faith meetings and discussions. There is much we can and ought to do. On the community and social level there are opportunities to engage in dialogue with people of other faiths on the level of better understanding and appreciation of what people believe. On the religious level, we can participate in discussion groups that specifically address the need for the various religions to be more inclusive in their thinking. Groups such as Progressive Christianity and Progressive Religious Thought provide such forums. Of particular relevance is the Parliament of the World's Religions (*www.cpwr.org*), which places great hope in change eventuating from below rather than from above.

Chapter 9

Renewal

? The overview of Church authority presented here is very negative. Alongside its mistakes, the Church has some great accomplishments in its missionary work, in ecumenism, in the promotion of scholarship, in health and education, and in social justice — to name just some. And Church authority in Rome has supported and encouraged those efforts.

There are many great accomplishments. The achievements, however, do not lessen the need for genuine reform in the Church, in its system of governance, in ritual, in spirituality, in the sacramental system and in the Church's official attitude to other religions.

? I cannot see how finding faults and criticizing the Church helps.

It is not a matter of finding faults. The concern is to see whether patterns of attitudes and behavior that fail to reflect the attitudes and behavior of Jesus are manifested by people exercising leadership roles in the Church. Discerning and clearly naming these patterns are vital for renewal of the Church. If they are not named, leadership will inevitably continue to adopt them to silence or disregard reforming voices.

What patterns are discernible?

So far we have seen reliance on a theological schema elevated to "certain knowledge" and considered beyond question. That remains in force today even though Jesus never used doctrinal statements as a requirement or a measure of discipleship. We have seen reliance on a concept of God that is elitist and exclusive and focuses on God at a distance from people. This concept has allowed and still allows Church leadership to view itself as custodians and dispensers of God's presence and favor. We have seen the use of force and punishment to control what Catholics think. That, too, remains in place today. The "force" may not be physical anymore but nonetheless is personally devastating for those theologians who find themselves under investigation. The systemic pressure on theologians to conform to what Rome thinks stifles free expression of what theologians might really be thinking.

Secrecy and anonymous reporting are part of that systemic pressure. We have seen Church leadership adopt quite extraordinary defense mechanisms against the insights of its own scholars. This includes the refusal to consider factual or scholarly data not in harmony with its theological thinking. We have seen scriptural literalism. Incredibly, we have seen the present pope, when he was in charge of the Congregation for the Doctrine of the Faith, argue that because some events are recorded in the Gospels they must thereby be historical fact. We have seen a consistent attitude from popes and other Church leaders that they do not have to listen to the voice of God in the people. That attitude still prevails in Church authority continuing to speak down to people and asserting it knows what God really thinks. We have seen elitism and arrogance in the way Catholic Church leadership proclaims its role in the world and among other religions. Despite much good work in missionary and ecumenical endeavors, this attitude stills underpins contemporary Church documents.

We have seen the Church, throughout its history, withstand procedures of open accountability. Church leadership considers it is accountable to no one except God — and it *knows* God thinks like it. All throughout its history, the Catholic Church has been dominated in its leadership and its decisions by males. And that male domination has been increased in recent centuries by an ever tighter system of centralized control. Rome rules the Church on all levels.

All of this comes under the heading of inappropriate patterns of attitude and behavior.

 I hear all that and find myself wondering what can I, an "ordinary" Catholic, do about it?

It is important that we do not allow ourselves to become locked into single issues, such as the ordination of women or homosexuality or a married clergy, and try to fight those issues on the terms in which Church authority chooses to deal with them. When we talk about issues that concern

us, let look us also for and name how Church leadership
at any level exhibits inappropriate patterns of attitudes and
behavior. It is important that we name what is going on;
otherwise Church leadership will bring the issues onto its
playing field, into its patterns, and the voices of renewal
will lose every time.

How will this work out in practice?

First, we need to look at the way Church authority presently handles issues about which we have concerns, to see
whether any of the patterns mentioned above operate,
and if they do, to promote open and honest discussion
about them.

That seems to be disloyal to the Church.

Church authority has every right to expect loyalty when
it operates according to Gospel values. It has no right to expect unquestioning loyalty when it uses tactics that would
embarrass Jesus.

And after this step of encouraging open discussion?

The next step is public articulation of how the situation
or issue could be handled differently if those inappropriate patterns were not brought to bear on it. This step is
the basic groundwork for genuine renewal in the Church.
Renewal is not just about change. It involves articulating
a solid theological foundation on which the changes need
to rest if they are to have acceptance.

Where do we start?

Well, if we made a list of issues on which we want to see some change or reform, what would you want to list?

- the sex abuse scandal and the way it has been handled

- shortage of priests

- celibacy

- right to Eucharist

- women's right to ordination

- women's voice

- election of bishops

- divorce and remarriage

- homosexuality

- abortion

- giving laity a voice

- religious fundamentalism

- boring liturgies

- patriarchy

- loss of the young

- fixation on sexual issues rather than broader social justice issues

- a constant invention of laws about how we worship on Sundays

- contraception

A common mistake is to take any of those issues separately and to press for change without realizing that Church authority has already set the limits and boundaries and context in which the case for change may be argued. It is the way those limits and context have been settled that needs challenging rather than expending time and energy seeking change within them. If this challenging is not done — and history tells us that Church authority will resist it and try to crush it — Rome will simply assert that change is not possible.

Let us apply this process to some of the issues listed.

Sexual Abuse Scandal

Many Catholics in the United States have had their trust in Church leadership shaken by research that revealed 5 percent of Catholic clergy and brothers have sexually abused minors. The percentage equates to three thousand offenders. Research also indicates that each offender averaged eight victims and thirty-two offenses. That is twenty-four thousand victims and ninety-six thousand incidents of criminal sexual abuse. These are only the reported figures. There is a high probability that these numbers represent only a small proportion of actual cases since clinical experience indicates that most victims do not report abuse. Eighty percent of the victims are post-pubescent boys (approximately thirteen to seventeen years of age). The offenders, strictly speaking, are ephebophiles rather than pedophiles. Pedophiles abuse pre-pubescent children.

Shocked and scandalized Catholics in the United States and in other countries asked how this could happen in their Church. That priests could engage in criminal sexual abuse seemed incomprehensible to people conditioned to think of priests as "men of God," above reproach. Their question is partly answered by reference to a clerical system that placed priests on a pedestal; by seminary training that removed men from social engagement with the world and was grossly deficient in helping young men, whether heterosexual or homosexual; adjust to their sexuality; by a clericalism that hid emotional immaturity behind a facade of having priestly powers; by a lack of proper psychological screening; and by the absence of adequate spiritual direction by competent guides. This was a system that not only allowed but abetted emotionally deprived men to reach ordination. It was a system that then protected them from accountability when doubts about their maturity and their behavior began to surface.

 What troubled me and other Catholics was not just that the abuse existed but that Church authority tried to cover it up.

That is why we must look for patterns of attitudes and behavior.

A key tactic used by Church authority was secrecy and cover-up. One reason Church officials resorted to such tactics was the need to protect the institution at all costs. What transpired was systemic denial of a problem, even when the U.S. bishops were warned quite explicitly in an address to their annual conference in Dallas in 1986 of its existence and its potential to do cause scandal and enormous financial harm to the Church. The denial also denied victims the right to a fair hearing and adequate treatment. Protecting the institution was more important for a significant number of bishops, rather than justice for victims or standing in genuine compassion with them.

 I know the sense of outrage in Boston was as much about the stonewalling from the cardinal and the attempts to hide the depth of the problem.

In response to the sexual scandal in the Boston Archdiocese, Catholics formed an organization, Voice of the Faithful, calling for greater accountability. VOTF gave people a platform on which they could be heard, and the organization experienced rapid growth throughout the United States and internationally. Its published goals are to support those who have been abused, to support priests of integrity,; and to shape structural change within the Church. Its motto is "Keep the Faith. Change the Church." Its mission is "to provide a prayerful voice, attentive to the Spirit, through which the Faithful can actively participate in the governance and guidance of the Catholic Church."

It is significant that VOTF expressly states in its official publicity: "VOTF does not seek any change in church doctrine. The problems which have come to light in the present crisis are more truly cultural than structural in nature."

It is significant because it immediately curtails VOTF as an effective long-term voice of reform. It means that

VOTF will not explore one of the most important questions that needs to be brought out into the open and discussed: What is the theological mind-set that makes bishops think they do not have to listen to the laity?

 Is that really such an important question?

Yes. Consider what happened to VOTF.

It did not take long for some bishops to reveal their paranoia about such a movement in their midst. In some dioceses, members of VOTF found themselves banned by bishops from holding meetings on Catholic property, despite VOTF's reassurance about not wanting to change doctrine. Why would bishops do that? They probably realized that any group seeking active participation "in the governance and guidance of the Catholic Church" would eventually realize there was more than either "cultural" or "structural" change involved.

Any close examination of the system of Church governance, the secrecy and the lack of accountability, would inevitably lead to an examination of the theology that transports some bishops into a rarefied ecclesial world adrift from the people they are supposed to serve. Aloof in their theological mind-set and in their security as "princes of the Church," these bishops let it be known they have no intention of allowing a lay voice to have a significant influence in Church governance. They also made it clear they are not answerable to the lay faithful. They adopted Rome's tactic of treating the faithful as "simple" people who need to be shielded from new ideas. The tactic keeps them well in control and helps them avoid any challenging questions.

Members of VOTF, publicly avowing not to criticize Church doctrine, now find themselves branded as "dissenters" and "disloyal." In effect, they have become victims of a classic Church tactic of demonizing reforming voices. Those bishops who assist the demonizing can now rest easy: This group not only *should* not be listened to, it *must* not be listened to.

Would VOTF be better off if it had opted to challenge Church doctrine?

Maybe not immediately so, since some of its members would not want to challenge doctrine. Yet, in the long run, it would be more beneficial as a voice of reform if it challenged its members to examine the doctrinal basis for bishops behaving as princely lords who cannot abide having their authority questioned. Ultimately, belief in where and how God's presence and "voice" are active in the Church has become a doctrinal issue.

How could doctrine determine the way a bishop acts?

The situation in Boston provides clues for an answer. Cardinal Bernard Law had the prestige of being the most influential power broker in the U.S. Church. Law would have resonated with Cardinal Ratzinger's prayer that bishops be "good merchants, faithful administrators of the goods with which we have been entrusted." He indicated this clearly in 1996 when he opposed other bishops calling for "dialogue" on "common ground" among Catholics. The only common ground, asserted Law, was "revealed truth or the authoritative teaching of the Church." Any "dialogue" dissenting from this "truth," said Law, was "deception."

In other words, bishops do not have to listen to the laity — in fact, must not listen — if they voice opinions contrary to the "truth" bishops have to guard?

Exactly. "Truth" has already been finalized and packaged. It is the role of bishops to tell the rest of the Church what this "truth" is. There is no room for dialogue here.

What does this have to do with the sex abuse scandal?

It has to do with power, with arrogance, with total lack of accountability, with immersing oneself in a theological mind-set that puts oneself above and beyond the reach of civil law, with lack of compassion for victims, with protection of the institution. It has to do with an absence of genuine pastoral concern, with acting as though "theological truth" and correct thinking are far more important than acting with the compassion and openness of Jesus. It has everything to do with not recognizing or giving consideration to God's presence in everyone. It is a theological mind-set that removes princes of the Church from engagement with the struggles, the questions, and the pain of Catholics in the pews.

If any of that sounds unfair, consider this. When Cardinal Law was pressured by public outcry to resign in disgrace, he moved to Rome where he was never asked by the pope or Vatican officials to resign from any of the official posts he held. Two of those positions involve the selection of bishops and handling the sexual abuse crisis. Then, on May 27, 2004, the pope appointed him as archpriest of St. Mary Major basilica. The position comes with a palatial apartment and a healthy stipend. It seems that neither the pope nor Vatican officials have any sense of the outrage against Law in the United States. It is far more likely that in their eyes he is a true loyal son of the Church. Why? Because he has always been a faithful defender of Church doctrine. That is what really counts for them, and for such he deserved to be honorably rewarded, not driven out of office in disgrace.

It seems that any time adherence to "correct thinking" or protecting the institution clash with acting decently or with compassionate pastoral concern or even with social justice, Church authority favors and rewards men loyal to the institution. Bishops know this. And some bishops play the system to their own advancement.

 Is Cardinal Law indicative of the mind-set operating in other bishops?

Possibly. It is a likely indicator why the U.S. bishops as a body ignored loud alarm bells that were ringing in the early 1980s. The *National Catholic Reporter* ran an article in 1983 warning of the magnitude of the problem and spoke of the "scandal" that the bishops had established no policies to address it. That particular scandal worsened when it became clear to Catholics almost twenty years later that it was the secular media that exposed the extent of the problem and the secrecy, the avoidance of due legal procedures, and the refusal of some bishops to be accountable to anyone.

 In fairness, it can be argued that the bishops did what they thought was right. They are not psychologists. They tried to address the problem as best they could.

No. That argument only serves to distract us from a crucial issue — the disastrous criteria used to select men to be suitable bishops. These men were elevated to the role of bishops because Roman Church authority considered they could be trusted to protect the "goods with which we have been entrusted," that is, the "truth" of Catholic doctrine. These men were not required to have pastoral expertise or any competence to deal with people issues. They were, and remain, willing participants in a system of governance that is manifestly incompetent in handling pastoral issues. As such, the system is an indictment on the state of leadership in the Catholic Church today. If we learn anything for the future governance of the Church from the sex abuse scandal, it will emerge from open and honest discussion about some basic questions: What is the role of a bishop in the Church? Who should be asked to undertake the role? How should the candidate be selected?

Aside from how bishops should be appointed, what are other practical issues that surface from the sexual abuse situation?

It seems a matter of priority that Church officials ensure that cases of criminal behavior receive no protection from Church structures and influence, but be handed over to civil authorities for investigation. It is easy to say, "If only . . ." in hindsight, but if this policy had been in place dioceses would not find themselves being sued for protecting priests who engaged in criminal behavior.

Church officials should readily comply with sex offenders' registration and notification laws where they exist, and advocate the passage of such laws where they do not exist.

While Church officials might take it for granted that a code of ethics governing interaction between clergy and youngsters is in place, they need to make this code more publicly explicit to ensure everyone knows there is such a code.

In keeping with the Church's sacramental practice of reconciliation — making amends for the harm done and being willing to do all it can to ensure the sin is eradicated — it is appropriate, even necessary, for the Church officials to sponsor psychological research to develop valid and reliable predictors of sexual abuse.

The Appointment of Bishops

The theological grounding for what became a patriarchal model of Church governance was established very early.

Ignatius of Antioch, writing about eighty years after the death of Jesus, taught that the bishop represented God. He went further, asserting that the bishop teaches with the authority of "God the Father"; he presides over his community "in God's place"; the faithful are to obey the bishop as they would obey God. This teaching gave enormous authority and prestige to bishops. However, the power it granted to bishops came at a great cost — the eventual abandonment of the early model of Church governance that took seriously the presence of God's Spirit operating in all members of the community.

In the early model of Church governance, bishops gained their teaching and leadership authority from the community in which they lived. It was the only way someone could be a bishop. He had to live in the community, and he had to be a recognized leader. Such a man could participate in the life of the community, could listen and learn and could ensure his teaching reflected the questions and issues confronting his community. In a real sense the community as "church" authorized him in his leadership position and consequently granted him enormous respect.

Over the centuries, the appointment of bishops in important dioceses became the concern of kings and princes, of politics, of bribery, of family interests, of power and influence. In spite of this, the traditional understanding of the community's role in electing its bishop or at least having a significant voice in his appointment was never lost — even though it was not translated into practice.

But is seems to be almost completely lost now.

After Vatican II there was considerable hope that Rome would be more respectful of the local Church community's participation in the selecting of bishops. That hope has been dashed. In recent years Rome has taken almost total control of the appointment of bishops throughout the world. The appointment of a bishop is now generally seen as something "Rome" or the pope does. Pope John Paul II made his pontificate the outstanding example of centralist control of this important aspect of Church life, with the local community having little or no voice.

 What criteria are used for making someone a bishop today?

The ultimate criteria for being elevated to a bishop have little to do with pastoral experience within the diocese in which the bishop is appointed leader. Loyalty to Rome and unquestioning acceptance of Rome's favored theology of salvation head the list. Rome has said as much in issuing the declaration *Dominus Iesus:* Rome looks for men who will "firmly believe and teach" the theology that is enshrined in that document. The prospective bishop must also promise never to allow public discussion of the issue of women becoming priests. He must promise to defend Rome's position against 80 percent of Catholics on the issue of contraception. Any candidate publicly advocating an end to enforced celibacy for priesthood can surrender any aspirations of becoming a bishop. And any bishop who publicly questions Roman policies does so at the expense of promotion to a larger or more influential diocese in the future.

 What about leadership in prayer, leadership of men and women, the ability to deal with challenging faith questions, witness to poverty, concern for social justice issues, displaying genuine heartfelt compassion with the broken people in our cities?

We do have some bishops of great leadership, vision, and courage in the Church today. The pity is that there are so few of them. The present system of appointment has promoted men who predominantly are men of the institution. The woeful handling of the sex abuse crisis is merely one indicator and symptom of that. For these men, the "Church" is not the body of faithful members. The "Church" is the institutional system of governance, and they have a privileged place in the system.

These men do not represent people; they do not represent the local faith community. They represent whoever is sitting in power in Rome. They look over their shoulders constantly to Rome, not daring to or not wanting to upset central control. They make little or no attempt to engage the faith questions of parents, priests, teachers, and adult faith educators. They are "answer" men, whose theological expertise is measured by their knowledge of the Catholic *Catechism*. They are fearful of any discussion or opinions that deviate from what they *know* to be "certain knowledge."

Inevitably they implement in their own dioceses the institutional system of fearful control in which the "watchdog" and reporting mentality is evident. Experienced adult faith educators find their fidelity to the Church being questioned on the basis of reports from people whose conventional faith is disturbed by new ideas. Teachers in Catholic schools find themselves wondering how they can teach the story of Adam and Eve with integrity when the bishop insists they must teach the "fall" as a "deed that took place." Catholics who join organizations seeking reform in the Church find themselves forbidden by the bishop to meet on Church property. Theologians who have signed an oath of fidelity stating, "I am committed to teach authentic Catholic doctrine" find their teaching position in some dioceses dependent on the approval of bishops whose theological competence is dubious. Priests find themselves being watched, reported, and questioned by diocesan administrators if they omit the Creed or if a secular song is played at a funeral.

Collectively such leadership can take the Church nowhere but backward. There can be no major reform within the Church, reform that will help the Church engage the disturbing faith questions of these times, without open and public criticism of the theology that drives the current system of selecting and rewarding bishops.

Pope John Paul II clearly understood his appointment of bishops around the world to be part of his legacy to the future Church, as the foundation on which the Church will stand strong.

Yes, he did. His legacy, however, is to lock the future Church into a theological worldview that is inadequate to deal with the faith questions of future generations of Catholics. Appointing men who will strenuously and loyally protect "the deposit of faith" may be an honorable intent, but in these times questions are being raised about the ability of a significant number of bishops to exercise genuine personal, spiritual, and pastoral leadership in the Church.

Who would want to be a bishop today? Surely the job description is too hard for anyone?

It depends on the "job description."

It might help if the emphasis on every bishop being primarily a defender of the faith were lessened. The emphasis has not succeeded in providing the Church with brilliant intellectual leadership from many bishops, and it has dismally failed to provide the Church with episcopal leaders with outstanding leadership qualities. If bishops were able to stop the pretense that they are experts in theology — those that are not experts, that is — and hand any concerns they have about theology to theological experts for advice, they might be more connected with the realities of life and the faith questions of the people they represent. Such connectedness would have to be an asset to the Church.

The bishop's role is basically a teaching role, though. That has always been the Church's tradition.

Yes, that is so, but the emphasis in the past one hundred years or so on being the teachers and guardians of a not-to-be-questioned theological schema has been at the expense of spiritual and pastoral leadership. That imbalance needs to be corrected if the Church is to have leadership in which Catholics can have confidence.

 I think there are broader issues connected with imbalance and leadership. I think clericalism, the nature of priesthood itself, and the lack of female representation in the Church are also part of the picture.

They are. Priesthood is a good starting point, since no other issue currently reflects so clearly how Catholics have been immersed in a theological mind-set that needs radical examination.

Priesthood

Garry Wills gives an excellent account of the "structures of deceit" operating in Rome in his book *Papal Sin*. He observes a recurring pattern in which "truth is subordinated to ecclesiastical tactics,"[21] such as attempts to show how Church teaching or accepted practice are faithful to the Scriptures while blatantly disregarding evidence from Scripture scholars to the contrary.

The tactics are intrinsically linked with the "God's plan of salvation" theology. They are clear for all to see in the way Rome handles the issue of priesthood.

Rome views Jesus through a theological understanding that developed well after Jesus died. St. Paul, for example, who never renounced his Judaism, knew nothing about a Trinitarian God. The earliest Christians, including St. Peter, did not proclaim that Jesus knew he was God incarnate. Instead, they preached that God did wonderful deeds through the "man" Jesus. The Acts of the Apostles has Peter proclaiming at Pentecost,

> Jesus the Nazarene was a man commended to you by God by the miracles and portents and signs that God worked through him when he was among you, as you all know. This man . . . you took and had crucified . . . but God raised him . . . God raised this man Jesus to life. (2:22–32)

Peter had no understanding of Jesus being God incarnate. Peter thought God raised the "man" Jesus into heaven, where God *"gave"* him "the Holy Spirit who was promised" and *then* "made him . . . both Lord and Christ" (2:36). "Lord and Christ" do not mean "God." A footnote in the Jerusalem Bible makes that clear. The context is also clear. God acted in and through Jesus. God rewarded Jesus. Jesus was the recipient of God's favor.

This raises an interesting question. Are we Catholic or Christian because we believe in doctrine? If so, neither Peter nor Paul belonged. Peter did not know Jesus was God incarnate, and Paul did not know God is a Trinity of persons.

Your comment highlights the imbalance we have in the Church today when fidelity to doctrine is made the test of whether someone is a loyal or "true" Catholic or not. Doctrine follows on from service and commitment. It is not an end in itself. It should not be the test of whether someone is "faithful" to following Jesus or not.

The other mistake, the one we are dealing with here, is to take for granted that Jesus acted according to doctrinal thought that developed well after he died. It is then not only presumed, but insisted upon as unquestionable, that Jesus *knew* he was the Second Person of the Trinity in human form and that he *knew* all of God's plans and that he *acted as God*.

I have always thought that. It seems to be basic Church teaching.

It is. And look what happens when that understanding is brought to the Last Supper. Catholic teaching presents Jesus as knowing God's plan and, based on John's Gospel, knowing he was to return to "heaven" from where he would send the Spirit down to earth. Catholics are taught to believe that Jesus "ordained" priests at the Last Supper, and if the word "ordained" is not used, then he "made" his apostles "priests" — even if the word "priest," as we use it today, is not used for them in Scripture. He knew he was setting up a new "Church" and he knew his "priests," acting like bishops (since being an apostle of Jesus automatically seems to give them "bishop" status), would ordain other priests and so "apostolic" succession would follow throughout the centuries. He made married men "priests," but the married factor is rarely mentioned because this action of Jesus conflicts with the Roman insistence on celibacy for priests. He changed bread and wine into his "body and blood" and gave his apostles the power to do this. He never gave this power, apparently, to his mother, so he thereby made it clear that women were to have no part in this new line of priesthood he was establishing.

This is the Jesus of "God's plan of salvation," setting up a new Church, with a new priesthood, to be the effective instruments of access to God through the sacraments. This is Pope Benedict XVI's "real Jesus of the Gospels," the "only savior, unique mediator," the Jesus who must be preserved at all costs.

 This is the Jesus we hear about every Holy Thursday. I never imagined I would ever question what I have heard and learned.

Why should Catholics ever stop to question it when it has been presented to them as reality — as Gospel fact? Most Catholics grew up imagining Jesus, the God-figure, at work at this meal. But, at the very least, as adults, they could examine the event on the level of human experience *before* the layers of theological interpretation are placed over it. When the layers of salvation theology are stripped away, when other scholarship is considered and brought to bear on the meal, a quite different reality is encountered. A Jewish man whose heart had been on fire with a dream

166

about God being present to everyone whatever the circumstances of their lives had a Passover meal with his Jewish friends. This Jew was not a priest. At a Jewish ritual, with his Jewish friends, he remembered with them the God who was faithful whatever the circumstances of life. He ate and drank this ritual meal with his Jewish companions and he apparently asked them to remember him in a special way whenever they, as Jews, gathered again to share this ritual meal that celebrated being God's covenant people.

Jesus ordained no one. There is no evidence in the New Testament that the apostles ordained anyone. There is no evidence in the New Testament that the followers of Jesus immediately after his death considered themselves members of a new religion. They were Jews. They gathered as Jews. They worshiped as Jews. They did not immediately set up a new cultic priesthood. The Acts of the Apostles presents these followers of Jesus as a group who "all lived together and owned everything in common," who "sold their goods and possessions and shared out the proceeds among themselves according to what each one needed. They went as a body to the Temple every day but met in their houses for the breaking of bread; they shared their food gladly and generously" (Acts 2:46).

The Scriptures cannot be much clearer that these followers of Jesus had no sense whatever of a priesthood distinct from Jewish practice. Church leadership asserts that Jesus ordained the apostles when the scriptural evidence suggests he did no such thing. Church leadership takes it for granted that Jesus established the Catholic Church despite the evidence that after Jesus' death his followers continued their daily visits to the temple.

This is a huge shift in thinking. I am not sure I either want to make it or can make it. It cuts across a lifelong pattern of belief about the Last Supper.

In that case, simply be open to the evidence and to where the evidence may take you.

Consider, for example, whether Jesus ever renounced his Jewish religion. Consider whether he ever gave any indication in his public preaching that he intended to start a breakaway religion. Consider how strange it is that Jesus should suddenly, without prior warning or preparation, "ordain" his apostles into a system of priesthood radically different from that of his own religion on the night before he died.

Maybe he did ordain his apostles, but they did not understand until later what he had done?

That is how Catholic teaching usually presents what happened. Pope John Paul II, in the introduction to his 2003 encyclical on the Eucharist, wrote:

Did the Apostles who took part in the Last Supper understand the meaning of the words spoken by Christ? Perhaps not. Those words would only be fully clear at the end of the *Triduum sacrum,* the time from

Thursday evening to Sunday morning.... This is already clear from the earliest images of the Church found in the Acts of the Apostles: "They devoted themselves to the Apostles' teaching and fellowship, to the breaking of bread and the prayers" (2:42). The "breaking of the bread" refers to the Eucharist.

The pope's reading of this text would have Catholics believe that the apostles came to an understanding of the "mystery of the Eucharist" on Easter Sunday and were celebrating Eucharist soon afterward. However, the breaking of the bread by this group of people still considering themselves faithful Jews does not refer to the Eucharist. This knowledge is available to anyone reading the footnote to this text in the Jerusalem Bible: "In itself the phrase suggests a Jewish meal at which the one who presides pronounces a blessing before dividing the bread."

The pope continued in his introduction,

The Son of God became man in order to restore all creation, in one supreme act of praise, to the One who made it from nothing. He, the Eternal High Priest who by the blood of his Cross entered the eternal sanctuary, thus gives back to the Creator and Father all creation redeemed. He does so through the priestly ministry of the Church, to the glory of the Most Holy Trinity.

This theological statement has little to do with reality. Dressing up a theological schema in grandiose language and using all the authority of a papal encyclical to teach it does not make it any more believable. The passage simply highlights the inability of Pope John Paul II's favored theology — and the theology of Catholic tradition — to speak to many twenty-first-century Catholics. The High Priest who sheds his blood to enter the eternal sanctuary? The High Priest who "gives back" to the Father "all creation redeemed"? While this language and imagery will continue to inspire some people, its continued use will ensure that traditional faith becomes more and more divorced from reality. The proponents of this theology are unwilling or unable to grasp the most basic faith questions: What are you asking people living in the twenty-first century to imagine? What are you talking about? What do you mean?

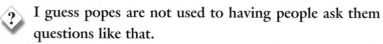

I guess popes are not used to having people ask them questions like that.

Nor are many bishops. Church leadership is not generally known for its willingness to expose itself to such questions.

If Jesus did not "ordain" anyone, what are the implications for priesthood as we know it today?

It questions the nature of priesthood. We have a well-developed cultic system of priesthood in the Church in which a man is given special powers to access the sacred when he is ordained. We have a well-developed sacramental theology that maintains that the Eucharist cannot be celebrated without that person being present to exercise the special power he has. That person need not have any leadership skills. He need not belong to the community. What is important, theologically, is that he is there to perform the action only he can perform. The system and the theology that underpins it make the laity dependent on a priest being present for the Eucharist to "happen." The focus is on the powers the priest has to make effective the presence of the Risen Jesus in the consecrated bread. The priest plays the role of mediator, effectively bringing the sacred presence to the community.

This is the theology that speaks of the priest being "another Christ," isn't it?

Yes. That is one reason that priests have been held in high respect in the Catholic community. They are deemed to have a connectedness with God that the laity do not have.

Is the respect for them misplaced?

It is if it is given solely on the grounds they hold a position of power. That would contradict the clear teaching of Jesus to his apostles about exercising leadership. Jesus clearly wanted respect to be earned from being of service to people, from not lording power and authority, from being compassionate, and from being identified with the "crowd" rather than being set apart from people.

What would Jesus think of the idea that priests have special powers to bring his risen presence to the community through the words of consecration?

Jesus the Jew would find the notion quite remote from anything he ever preached or did. His preaching focused on God, not himself. His preaching about God emphasized the importance for people to recognize God's presence in their everyday activities. Apart from the theology developed in John's Gospel well after Jesus' death, the Gospels present Jesus as revealer of God's presence *with* people, not as the mediator who brought God's presence to them. The Jesus who preached about the kingdom of God in our midst would undoubtedly be mystified by a religion bearing his name that made people dependent on men with special powers to bring God's presence to them.

? Would Jesus, then, be more at home with a ritual that celebrated God's presence with people rather than a ritual that focused on God coming to them through the special powers a priest has?

Jesus, the Jew, certainly would be. The Passover meal was a celebration of God with the Jewish people in their history and in their personal lives. It had nothing to do with someone with special powers to bring God's presence to the table.

? I sometimes find myself at Sunday Mass shaking my head and asking myself, "What has this got to do with what Jesus did at the Last Supper?"

That is a crucial question if the Church wants to trace priesthood back to that meal. What stands out about the meal is the richness and the abundance of symbol and how symbols were used in a striking way to capture belief in the God who journeyed with people in the good and the hard times. The people remembered the past to strengthen their belief in God with them in the present. That is an essential pattern of Jewish prayer.

The symbols, such as the bitter herbs, the bread, and the wine, were part of the story that was told. People present were told why they ate bitter herbs, why they drank wine and ate bread. What they did not do was ask how the symbols worked or how God became present in and through them, or who had special powers to make God present in them. Jesus never did that. Jews did not do that. It took the Christian religion to distrust the power of symbol, to objectify symbols, to have intense arguments over how a presence "came" to them and then to legislate about who had the power to make this happen properly. Jesus would never have done that.

 I cannot imagine any of the apostles at the Last Supper wondering just how Jesus' "body" got into the bread.

Precisely. That sort of thinking, which later necessitated the Church's teaching on transubstantiation, had no place in the Jewish approach to symbols.

"Transubstantiation" has more to do with mental gymnastics than with reality. It is a Middle Age answer to questions that should never be asked, such as: How does the presence of Jesus come into the bread? What happens to the bread if there is a "real" change? They are the wrong questions to ask about a sacrament. It would be like asking how the presence of God comes into the water used at baptism to make that sacrament effective. The inevitable result of that approach to the sacraments, evident in Vatican decrees, is a fixation about the physical matter — what it must be, how it works, who can control it — rather than the disposition and character of the people involved in the action.

 I cannot imagine Jesus being concerned — as the Vatican clearly is — about the actual wheat content of the bread for it to be effective as a symbol.

That comments raises two issues. The first is the Catholic Church's insistence that the consecrated bread is "not merely" a symbol. The Church constantly uses "really and truly" language about the "body" of Jesus being present. This, in turn, causes enormous confusion about the difference between a physical presence of Jesus (which it is not) and a sacramental presence (which it is). Yet the "really and truly" language the Church uses would have Catholics believe it is "not merely" a sacramental presence. The language pushes the Catholic imagination toward a physical reality, especially when it goes hand in hand with Church teaching about a "change of substance" — transubstantiation — at the consecration.

The second issue is the Church's insistence that the sacrament is ineffective if there is not some wheat in the bread. In August 2004 the Vatican reiterated its ban on gluten-free wafers, insisting that the eucharistic bread must contain some wheat. This ban effectively denies access to Communion in the form of bread for all sufferers of coeliac disease, who are allergic to wheat. Presumably, the Vatican believes the presence of the risen Jesus cannot "come" into the bread unless some wheat is present. The issue demonstrates the absurdity to which the Vatican is prepared to move in order to protect its theology. That theology locates the presence of God more in a wafer having wheat than one not having wheat. It also places the focus in eucharistic theology more on the bread and how it works and who has power to make it work than on people trying to live the reality of *being* "the body of Christ."

 Where does that leave us with Communion, then?

It leaves us where it should leave us — on the powerful level of symbol. Take, for example, as someone mentioned earlier, the symbol of wearing a wedding ring. It is the wearing of it and what the ring symbolizes that are important. The wearer pledges to be faithful to what the giving and the wearing of the ring symbolize: fidelity, commitment, permanent bonding. The ring is given only when its wearer personally commits to be faithful to what the wearing of the ring symbolizes. If the wearer were to cheat on the partner, the ring would lose its meaning. The ring's value is not in its physical makeup. We do not ask how love "gets into" the ring. That would be asking the wrong question about the symbol. We do not insist that unless the ring has a definite gold content it cannot effectively symbolize the bond of love between two people.

Communion should be like that. We gather to hear the story of Jesus. We want to pledge our willingness and our commitment to allowing the Spirit that moved in him to move in us. The crucial issue is: to what are we committing ourselves if we gather around the story of Jesus and eat this bread in memory of him? We should make that commitment quite explicit — just as a couple do when they exchange rings. The focus in Communion should not be on receiving something or someone. It should be on committing ourselves to *be* someone.

 Should the Catholic Church continue to deny Communion to non-Catholics?

No. At a wedding the couple are asked to pledge commitment to mutual love. When they do that, they exchange rings. A couple would be puzzled beyond belief if the celebrant insisted they could not exchange rings unless they could give assent to how the ring actually worked. But that's what the Catholic Church does with Communion. It is not concerned whether other Christians are willing to publicly pledge their commitment to following Jesus. No, the focus is on what people believe about how Jesus actually becomes present in the bread. That focus is narrow, divisive, and exclusive. As such, it can only be presented in the name of a narrow, divisive, and exclusive voice — never in the name of Jesus.

 But this is all very Protestant!

Catholics, generally, are conditioned to believe that at the time of the Reformation the reformers were wrong

176

about everything. We have inherited a deep-seated attitude of distrust about Protestant theology. We need to remind ourselves that some of the best thinkers among the reformers were what we would regard as former "Catholic" scholars. The Reformation period was a time of great bitterness, distrust and violence. It has taken hundreds of years for scholars on both sides to come together for discussions held with mutual respect. This will happen more and more as both Catholic and Protestant theologians accept the need to abandon a theological schema of salvation that is not relevant for these times. When this happens, open discussion on how symbols work and how far removed anything Jesus did at the Last Supper is from present Catholic eucharistic and priestly theology and practice will also be on the agenda. There will come a day when the Vatican and the Catholic hierarchy will not be able to avoid or silence those discussions. So, far from being fearful of Protestant theology, we should look forward to how open dialogue and mutual trust might renew the Church.

 What, then, is the role of priesthood?

Priesthood should be a position of leadership to call us into the truth of who we are as we gather around the story of Jesus. It should not be the role of go-between, a mediator between God and people. Priesthood should be freed from the theology that requires priests to have powers lacking in the laity to access the sacred. The priestly role is not to bring God's presence to people. It should be modeled on Jesus' example of affirming God's presence in people.

The priest's sacramental ministry should emphasize God's presence in people. The role should be people-centered, not theology-centered. Anyone exercising the position should have evident skills in leading a community and be respected for such. The powers-granted model of priesthood is too commonly a recipe for dysfunctional community life. We all know too many priests who consider themselves un-accountable, have no leadership skills, hide behind their clerical powers, and refuse to do any in-service. In any other professional field such men would not survive, but priesthood is a haven for these men because they have special powers granted in ordination — and Catholic communities the world over are dependent on them for the Eucharist.

The best priests — we can all test this — are men of wisdom, leadership, integrity, and spirit. And there is no reason that a renewed concept of priesthood, based on leadership qualities, could not include women.

 How might we effectively break from the present system of clerical control?

The most effective means at present is for Catholics to gather in small groups to discuss their faith and to ritualize it — while maintaining contact on the parish level of community. These small groups can explore and experiment with ritual language that is not linked with fall-redemption theology. They can find language that is more expressive of God's universal presence. People can gather around the story of Jesus and in sharing bread and wine in his memory commit themselves to allow the Spirit that moved so freely in Jesus' life to be expressed more generously in their lives.

? We have to stop being dependent on a priestly caste to bring the sacred to us?

Definitely. Let us shift from theology and ritual that insist priests are necessary for bringing God's presence to people's lives. Let us explore what it means to be living *in* love and *in* God — and the role of the priest in this task.

? What is being expressed here brings a different perspective to the issue of women's ordination in the Catholic Church.

Yes. If the role of priesthood were to change, then there is no question that women could participate on an equal footing with men. It would be a great blessing for the Church community to have women exercising their leadership skills.

? But Rome takes the view that it cannot change what God has established. It has no power whatever to change the role or the banning of women.

This is the tactic Rome likes to use: God planned this; we cannot change it. It is a classic example of Rome trying to lock the rest of the Church into its biased theological thinking and insisting its decisions cannot be questioned.

What Jesus did at the Last Supper has no bearing on whether women should be ordained priests today, since we are dealing today with a priestly structure and theology unknown to Jesus and his apostles.

Pope John Paul II, however, felt free to totally ignore any data like this that might undermine the theological schema he brought into play when pontificating on issues relating to priesthood. The pope's apostolic letter *Ordinatio Sacerdotalis*, issued at Pentecost in 1994, is a classic example of the Roman mind-set at work. The first words set the scene: "Priestly ordination, which hands on the office entrusted by Christ to his Apostles of teaching, sanctifying and governing the faithful..." It is clear, however, from the Acts of the Apostles that the early followers of Jesus would have no idea of what the pope is talking about in linking "priestly ordination" and "office" with the apostles — who clearly went to the Temple to pray (Acts 3:1). The development of a specific Christian system of priesthood had more to do with later Christians separating from Judaism than anything Jesus, the Jew, did at the Last Supper or anything the first Christians did when they met to remember Jesus.

The pope stated early in the encyclical, "the exclusion of women from the priesthood is in accordance with God's plan for his Church." Here is that Roman tactic at work again — invoking "God's plan for..." in an attempt to prevent or end discussion. Far from doing either, it raises a basic question: Just what understanding of God did the pope have? The question has importance both in this context and when the pope exhorted people in the midst of the hot European summer of 2003 to pray to God that "He" send rain. Catholics wrestling with important issues, such as priesthood in the Church, have the right to expect that the head of their Church and cardinals and archbishops cease invoking a first-century concept of an interventionist God with a "plan" to end all discussion.

The pope invoked God's "plan" again in trying to explain why Mary did not receive the office of "ministerial priesthood":

> Furthermore, the fact that the Blessed Virgin Mary, Mother of God and Mother of the Church, received neither the mission proper to the Apostles nor the ministerial priesthood clearly shows that the non-admission of women to priestly ordination cannot mean that women are of lesser dignity, nor can it be construed as discrimination against them. Rather, it is to be seen as the faithful observance of a plan to be ascribed to the wisdom of the Lord of the universe. (no. 3)

 It amazes me to think that in this day and age we are being asked to believe in a "Lord of the universe" who actually thinks about and sets up plans for human activities!

Yes, but if you can invoke the "Lord of the universe" on your side, then you can legislate in His name and decree that this is *never* to be challenged. The pope remarked that the issue of women priests "at the present time in some places is nonetheless considered still open to debate" and that "the Church's judgment that women are not to be admitted to ordination is considered to have a merely disciplinary force." He then decreed:

> Wherefore, in order that all doubt may be removed re-garding a matter of great importance, a matter which pertains to the Church's divine constitution itself, in virtue of my ministry of confirming the brethren (cf. Luke 22:32), I declare that the Church has no au-thority whatsoever to confer priestly ordination on women and that this judgment is to be definitively held by all the Church's faithful. (no. 4)

A year later, in November 1995, the Congregation for the Doctrine of the Faith declared that this ruling of the pope was to be regarded as an "infallible" teaching.

Rome decreed that Catholics were forbidden to dis-cuss the matter publicly and bishops were commanded to enforce the ban.

 I suspect most Catholics like me have no idea of what goes on behind the scenes with issues such as this. I've always trusted that the pope and the highest teaching authorities in the Church have access to truth in a way I haven't. It would never have crossed my mind to think they would use dubious tactics and misrepresentation of data to protect their entrenched thinking.

That is why it is so important to bring out into the open the theological schema that drives their thinking and motivates them to act like this.

Many Catholics no longer give credence to the notion of God that underpins that theological schema. They have replaced it with respect for a universal presence moving in the minds and hearts and lives of all people. These Catholics can scarcely believe the audacity of men in Rome who, with all the ecclesial power they can muster, tell them they are not even allowed to speak in public about ordination of women. Their amazement is matched by their disappointment in their local bishops who lamely acquiesce to Rome's dictates in the name of "loyalty" and "fidelity" or for the sake of their own ecclesial career path.

If we shift ground so radically on the way we discuss women's ordination, it would seem necessary also to free discussion about priestly celibacy from the traditional theological perspective in which it has been discussed.

The celibacy issue also provides insights into the mindset and tactics adopted by Vatican authorities.

Most Catholics believe the time has come for the Church to change its law on mandatory celibacy for priests. Some of the bishops at Vatican II wanted the issue discussed, only to have Pope Paul VI ban any discussion. It was not opportune, he said, for the bishops to be discussing such an important topic, a topic that needed much "prudence." Since the tactic of banning discussion worked so well for him, it has been repeated ever since, with Roman authorities repeatedly removing the topic from the agenda at any gathering of bishops.

Pope Paul VI later wrote an encyclical on priestly celibacy. The encyclical and other statements from Rome on the topic in the past forty years reveal:

+ A refusal to consider scriptural passages that clearly contradict the position being taken; for example, Paul's statement that he has a "right to take a Christian woman" around with him like "all the other apostles," but has not exercised his right (1 Cor. 9:5).

+ A distortion of scriptural passages to "prove" Jesus intended the position being taken by Rome. Yet it is clear that Jesus never chose celibate men to be his apostles. It is clear that Jesus never intended to begin a new type of priesthood. It is clear that the first Christians had no concept of a new type of priesthood. Whatever Jesus said about being "better not to marry at all" (Matt. 19:10) had no reference whatever in Jesus' mind or in the minds of his listeners to the issue of a celibate priesthood.

+ The insistence that this is what "God wants." Pope John Paul II, in his *Exhortation to the Church in Europe,* wrote, "Celibacy is not merely an ecclesiastical discipline imposed by authority; rather it is first and foremost a grace, a priceless gift of God for his Church." Presumably no one should argue against God's grant of a "priceless gift" to "his" Church.

+ Confusing the issue. No one would argue that celibacy, freely chosen, as seems to have been the case with Jesus, is a precious gift of one's life for the sake of others.

However, this should never be confused with the issue of mandatory celibacy. Men generally choose priesthood and accept celibacy as the price to be paid, whatever the theological and spiritual interpretations they receive in the seminary. And men ordained in their mid- to late twenties, shielded as they have been in their seminary years from the give-and-take of normal relationships with women, have no real idea of the psychological and personal price they are being asked to pay in accepting to be celibate. For many, if not most priests, celibacy is a cost to be paid for giving one's life to the Church in ministerial priesthood. It is not a gift. It is a burden. Surveys reveal that many priests are not faithful to what is entailed.

- Valuing their position on mandatory celibacy being of greater importance than the right of all Catholic communities to eucharistic celebration. There is little sense in invoking Scripture and Church tradition for convoluted support for mandatory celibacy while ignoring the fact that Christians in the early centuries of the Church would be amazed and even scandalized at the notion that a Christian community could not have eucharistic celebrations.

- Protecting the Church's teaching at all cost. The clear intent is to be guardians, "faithful administrators," of the status quo. It seems no pope wants to be remembered as the pope who changed what was fiercely defended as God's priceless gift to the Church. The tactic is to resist talk of the "signs of the times" as a temptation to deviate from God's "plan" for "His" Church.

• Fear. Below the surface is the fear of not being able to control a system of married priests the way the present system of celibate priesthood is tightly controlled.

Institutional leadership cannot afford, it seems, to allow any change that would call into question its ability to discern the mind and "plan" of God not only on the nature of priesthood, but also on other issues of "great importance" such as contraception, homosexuality, divorce and remarriage, or the use of condoms in AIDS-stricken countries.

People concerned with these issues should draw attention to the theology that allows Church leaders to disregard their experience and their opinions. The public questioning of this theology is the key to any genuine Church reform. Only when this theology is explored publicly and thoroughly will people see the ruination and harm it causes not only people in their personal relationships but also the Church in general.

The Church and Women

I would like to see more public education on and questioning about the Catholic Church's attitude toward women. I acknowledge that the attitude is changing significantly in various parts of the Church, like in my own diocese, but it seems that the institutional Church

is dragging centuries of theological and cultural baggage about women along with it and that this baggage needs to be publicly exposed if it is to cease having influence.

Several items stand out. One is the notion of woman as "temptress," not to be trusted. Another is the notion of woman as subordinate to man. All throughout its history, the Church has treated women with suspicion and with belief in male superiority. Medieval scholars, including Thomas Aquinas, taught that women do not have the wisdom of men and therefore should not be entrusted with public office in the Church. Moreover, these scholars taught, women in public office were liable to stir lust in men.

It is interesting to look at what the Church tradition did to Mary. It basically stripped her of womanhood. Yes, there is lip service to Mary, woman and mother, but she is basically sexless, beyond temptation, ageless, obedient, perfect, the "ark of the covenant," "mystic rose," "tower of David." She is an unreal projection of male theology.

How influential are the negative attitudes today? Look at a totally male hierarchy and ask what is the theological reasoning for totally excluding women. The basic answer: women cannot represent God as well or as fittingly as men can. This reasoning, of course, is based on the traditional salvation theology. Only men can properly represent God-as-revealed-in-Jesus. God is obviously male. A male hierarchy must even be the fruit of God's plan for "His" Church. This must not, indeed, cannot, ever be changed.

This line of thinking is still being regularly heard from members of the hierarchy.

? The difficulty many of us experience these days is what to believe and whom to believe when so much is changing. There is also the issue of who are we to question the Church. We are not theologians.

It is unnerving for many Catholics and other Christians also to find the ground of their faith shifting underneath them. One of the instinctive reactions is to seek an immediate new package of faith that will answer all the questions being raised — and that is not possible. The reality is that we will have to live with more ambiguity and unanswered questions than ever before. What is important is that we do not evade the challenge of bringing our experience of life, our questions and our knowledge about our universe to an articulation of what we believe as adults. We are not professional theologians, but our questions are just as valid as anyone else's and we have to take some responsibility for what we believe as adults. Add to this the fact that Catholic theologians are restrained by Church authority from speaking publicly on issues the way we would like them to, and it becomes even more vital that we accept the challenge we face.

The challenge, however, may not be as daunting as it first seems, provided we articulate clearly the ground on which we choose to stand in a time of extraordinary change.

Chapter 10

Solid Ground
on Which to Stand

We believe in a reality we call "God." That is our starting point. We believe this reality is everywhere, holding everything in existence. We acknowledge that this reality is beyond any images we can construct and beyond anything our words might describe. We no longer think of this reality the way people of ancient times thought of a God in the heavens looking down on earth. This reality is not a male divine being residing somewhere in outer space. We believe this reality is a universal presence holding all things in connectedness and relationship. This reality is not more present in one place than somewhere else. And everything that exists gives expression in its own way to this reality.

This reality has been creatively present in every atom, in every object, in every plant and animal, and in every person on this planet since it first took shape.

We believe that the human species gives a particularly wonderful expression to this reality since, in this life-form, the reality we call "God" can speak and sing, dance and interact in ways seemingly unique in the entire universe. Every person on this planet gives expression to God in his or her own unique way.

We believe that the best possible expression the human species can give to this reality is found in the endeavor to live in connectedness and right relationships.

We recognize our widespread human failure to live in respectful connectedness with one another and with the planet that nurtures and sustains us. We know only too well that the human species has yet to develop a collective consciousness that strives for unity and nobility. We are aware of the fear, the ignorance, the prejudices, the greed, the selfishness, and the desire to control and dominate others that create divisions between people.

We gather around the story of Jesus because we believe this story opens our minds and eyes to what could be possible if the human species truly realized how the shared experience of love is a pointer to the universally shared connection with the mysterious presence we Christians call "God." This story calls each of us to be the best possible expression of that presence we can be. It calls us to shape community and human interaction conscious that all people are intimately connected with God, whatever their religious beliefs. It is a call to end religious divisions based on the human need to be "right" or on men having special powers to access the sacred.

This is solid ground on which to stand as we contemplate the task of renewal in the Church.

I would like to probe more whether God is personal or not. I hear you indicating that you no longer believe in a personal God, yet I cannot see myself giving up the notion of a personal God. That seems to take all the ground away from me rather than giving me ground on which to stand. Do you think God is impersonal? I mean, is God conscious of being God? Is God intelligent? Does God know anything? Or do we just have this impersonal, mysterious reality we know nothing about, and it knows nothing about us?

The issue is not whether God is "personal"; the issue is whether God is beyond all our human categories, no matter how noble, dignified, or even meaningful they may be for us. Rather than defend the notion that God is personal, we should be asserting that God is beyond whatever our human understanding of "personal" is. If we consistently fail to do this — as we do — we imagine a God who acts, thinks, plans, and reacts the way a "person" does. We have seen this again and again in these pages: the God who has a plan, the God who sends His Son, the God who chooses, the God who rewards.

By all means let people hold on to a "personal" God as a way of relating with a mystery, but let them also accept that our experience of what "personal" means in no way describes God, nor must this human characteristic be an essential attribute of God.

Think of the size of our universe. We cannot comprehend its size. Consider that there may be many universes. Acknowledge in this context that "God is everywhere."

191

So what sense can we make of a "Person" co-extensive with and beyond the realm of multiple universes? If we want to assert that "God is a Person," we must at the same time acknowledge that this "Person" is not localized somewhere, as any person we know is. Let us not think of God as a deity or a supreme being in heaven or anything like that.

One way around that difficulty might be to refer to God as "Cosmic Mind." That might also help us with dealing with whether God is conscious of knowing.

That title may help as long as "mind" refers to a mysterious force, presence, or power holding everything in connectedness and relationship. The difficulty is that we too easily slip back into imagining a Mind that thinks, plans, and arranges much as a human mind operates.

I still cannot see what is wrong with having a God who thinks, notices, plans, loves, and cares.

We have to come to terms with the fact that this notion of God is a human construct, the product of how a particular life-form with conscious awareness on a planet in a cosmic nowhere thinks and views the universe. We cannot and should not try to contain whatever God is within the boundaries of our human experiences of thinking, noticing, and planning. At the very least, let us make some sincere efforts to shift from notions of a God who thinks and acts like the human species thinks and acts.

How does what you are saying relate with the scriptural statement "God is Love"? Is it helpful to keep saying that God is Love?

It is on a par with Jesus calling God "Abba" ("most loving father"). Neither is a description of God. Both titles are used to point to a relationship of trust. In other words, whatever God is, relate with God trustingly. Love is of paramount importance because we believe that our loving gives the best possible expression to the mystery we call "God." That's what the life and teaching of Jesus reveal for us.

Calling God "Love," though, creates the same difficulty as "Person" or "Cosmic Mind." It sets up images of a deity constantly immersed in value judgments and value reactions in line with human behavior, for example, a God moved to mercy and compassion. It is a simple step from there to imagine that God watches and notices, that God is moved by human activity, that God has opinions, that God legislates, that God rewards or punishes. All of this is a projection of how human beings operate through value judgments and reactions. Basically it all points to a God thinking and acting like we think and act, no matter how often and how strongly we assert that God is "beyond" our ways of thinking and acting.

 But surely God thinks and acts!

That is a good example of how our language keeps misleading us: God thinks and acts. What are we imagining?

193

Does God think about something for a while and then decide to act? That is how we operate. We receive data and information, process it, then decide on an action. And that is definitely not how God operates — unless you want to restrict God to a human operational mode. We, however, influenced by a lifetime of imagining that God hears our prayers and decides whether to answer them or not, keep thinking God operates this way. Or we are influenced by thoughts of God watching over the earth and deciding what actions to take in response to what is happening.

It is an important issue that we need to talk about more if we want to be consistent in shifting from belief in an overseeing deity to belief in God as a universal presence. That presence need not — and does not — "think about" things.

One way to appreciate the difference between the way this presence operates and the way we operate in our thinking and action is to consider energy — the all-pervasive phenomenon throughout the universe from the subatomic world through to the galactic arena. Energy goes hand in hand with action and with relationships and connectedness and outcomes. Yet there need not be any conscious thinking process present in almost all of this activity. Human thinking is the one exception we know of. Does that mean our thinking process is superior to the way energy operates all through the universe? No, our way of receiving sensory data and consciously processing it is but one way this phenomenon comes to expression when conditions produce a particular life-form.

Maybe "God is Energy" would be more apt than "God is Love"?

At least we could say that reflection on energy can lead or point us to an enriched understanding of God. It could alert everyone to the everywhere presence of God. It could help us appreciate such important aspects as universality, awesomeness, power, process, development, sustenance, connectedness, relatedness, possibility, and so on. It would help put an end to a theological mind-set whereby religious institutions claim to have unique access to the reality.

It seems to me that we should stop using the word "God." There is no longer any uniform understanding, meaning, or image to which the word points.

Many Christians would agree with you. One of the problems with the word is the fact it is the singular form of "gods" — and gods came before God. How do we think of or imagine gods? Usually they are like glorified or divine persons with great powers who live in the heavens. God then emerged in human thought as the greatest, the most powerful god, and then into the one and only God. It was inevitable that "God" carried the connotations of an all-powerful supreme deity in heaven who controlled everything.

An unfortunate consequence of this development is that discussion about whether God exists or not has commonly been about this supreme deity, and any denial of the existence of this deity shocks Christians. The discussion would be more fruitful if we changed the starting point from debating whether God exists to thoughtful reflection on the nature of the universe. That reflection could consider whether the universe carries within itself, at all levels, a psychic-spiritual dimension beyond mere physicality; whether order, relationship, and connectedness are evident at all levels of existence; and whether we could and should use our human term "intelligence" for any of this. Then we could reflect on where such reflections lead our thinking. It will not lead many Christians anymore to a deity who is an intelligent designer and master of the universe, but it will lead many who reject that notion of God to renewed appreciation of "God" as a power and presence beyond all our human images and ideas. The appreciation of Jesus as revealer of the presence in our living and loving will increase, as will appreciation of the wonderful life-form we are and our connectedness with all of humanity, with our planet, and with the entire universe.

 We need to use a name or title to replace "God," though.

The difficulty is finding a replacement that people are comfortable with, one that avoids the personalizing or literalizing of our human language and concepts. Some worthwhile suggestion are "the Divine," "Ultimate Mystery," and "Ground of all being."

Let us try using "the Divine." Immediately, some people will ask what is meant by the word. They want a clear definition, as if the definition will adequately describe the mystery to which the word points. Such a demand needs

196

to be resisted. The Divine is not a title. It is not a name. It is a word that could point to a mystery beyond all titles, names, and descriptions.

So we could say: the Divine permeates all of reality; the Divine comes to expression in all people in and through their loving; Jesus revealed our intimate connection with the Divine; prayer is meant to deepen our awareness of our connectedness with the Divine; sacraments celebrate the divine presence and challenge us to give witness to that presence; we are never separated from the Divine; the Church exists to preach the good news that all people, everywhere are connected in the Divine; the human task is to discern how attention to the divine presence within all people could lead us to greater respect for one another and to increased care for this planet and the environment.

We realize we are struggling with words here, but at least the attempt honors a universal presence and avoids a religious mind-set anchored in notions of exclusive access to an elsewhere God.

 Are we, then, "divine" in the way Jesus was divine?

Definitely. As we saw earlier, this was the whole point of Jesus' preaching — to elevate our understanding of ourselves by becoming aware of our intimate connection with the Divine. The Christian Church changed the focus by separating the Divine from the human and then arguing that Jesus had to have a special share in the Divine in order to bridge the gap between the two.

Does the word "sacred" lose all meaning if everything shares in the Divine?

The meaning and importance generally given to "sacred" have their origins in the artificial split between the Divine and the human. Christianity has highlighted that split in its doctrine about Jesus as the unique savior of the world and in its sacramental theology and practice. Think of the tabernacle in Catholic churches. Catholics have been conditioned to believe that is where the sacred really is. What if we believed that we and the entire world were equally permeated with the presence of the Divine? How would we relate with each other and with planet Earth?

By all means let us retain the word "sacred," but preferably in the understanding that in this place, object, or person the Divine has been wonderfully manifested, not in the sense that this or that is sacred and we and the rest of the universe are not.

 I'm trying to immerse myself in thinking about God as a universal presence, something like a reality that binds and holds everything together, something beyond all imagining. As I try to follow through with this thinking, especially about not personalizing God into human categories, I'm wondering what I, as a Christian, do with the doctrine of God as three Persons in One. I've been told I can no longer call myself a Christian if I do not believe in the Trinity.

Christian doctrine has made belief in three Persons in One necessary, as if a denial of this belief would undermine the Christian religion. As we saw earlier, the earliest Christians did not have this belief. If the belief was so essential to Christian living, we might expect that Jesus would have spent considerable time and effort expounding this doctrine to his followers.

 Is belief in the Trinity, then, an optional belief for Christians?

Of course it is, despite institutional Church authority and most Christian theologians insisting it is not. There is no evidence to suggest Jesus made belief in a Trinitarian God a requirement for his followers.

Keep in mind that three core issues led to the development of Trinitarian thought in the Christian community. First, the dualistic understanding of the separation between heaven and earth. Second, the belief that through Adam's sin humanity lost access to that place, heaven, where God dwelled. Third, asking who Jesus had to be in order to gain access to God's dwelling place.

If the Christian religion wants to continue insisting that Jesus has to be "truly God and truly man" and thereby make belief in God as a Trinity of Persons necessary, then it can no longer rely on any of those three foundational issues to make its case. They are no longer credible. Why build faith on sand?

But Jesus said, "The Father and I are one."

The statement is found in John's Gospel, which, as we have seen, appeared generations after Jesus died. The words put onto Jesus' lips present a theology that developed after Jesus died. They cannot be used to prove that Jesus knew about a Trinity of Persons in God, even less to prove that he knew he was the incarnation of one of them.

It seems to me you can no longer call yourself a Catholic. Your thinking is more in line with Unitarian thought than Catholic Church doctrine.

I'm sure some other Catholics would agree with you. The bottom line, however, is not where I belong. It is whether the Catholic Church should engage in some honest and open discussion about key issues on which its doctrines are grounded. And genuine dialogue with Christians such as the Unitarians would reveal that commitment to the life and teaching of Jesus would not be undermined if those issues are critically examined. The dialogue would also shed much needed light on what is essential to being a "Christian" or a "Catholic."

I have always imagined that when I die I will meet God and that there will be an embrace like Jesus described in the story of the prodigal son returning to his father. I can adjust to accepting there will not be an actual embrace, person to person, but I am sensing more ground shifting from beneath me as I follow through with this thinking. I'm wondering now whether God will even notice my death. This is a huge step for me to take — and I am not sure I want to take it.

Who knows what is on the other side of death and what it is like? As Christians we rely on the teaching of Jesus, especially through his stories, that we have nothing to fear in death if we have visited, cared, shared, and done our best to live decent lives. Death will be like that embrace you mention. It will be a transformation into another way of living on in that ultimate mystery — a way beyond all our thoughts and images, a way beyond our human way of knowing. We can still face death with the confidence of this faith even as we acknowledge the need to stop locking that ultimate mystery into noticing and acting in terms of our human way of noticing and acting.

 I still cling to a belief that justice and an afterlife are connected. I cannot believe that evil people are not called to account somehow, somewhere if they die without being called to account here on earth.

The concept of judgment and punishment after death has a long history in religious thought, especially within Christianity, doubtless because we all want to see evil people brought to justice. A basic flaw in the concept, though, is that it stresses the "next life" and puts the task on a personal God to bring people to justice. That simply sidesteps the fundamental issue: justice is a human responsibility. Jesus, along with other great religious leaders, would remind us that it is our task to create peaceful and just societies and to incorporate systems of accountability into our achievements. If this is not happening, then we need to examine what we, collectively, are doing wrong, rather than pinning our hopes on the next life. In particular we need to shift our focus in the Western world from individual sin — while not overlooking that — onto the systemic evil rampant in corrupt political wheeling and dealing with profit-hungry powerbrokers, in corporate greed, in military spending, in the abuse of natural resources, and in the obsession with wealth and comfort while more than half the world lives below the poverty line, to name just a few areas of concern. We should also examine the extent to which institutionalized religion causes distrust, fear, divisions, wars, and persecutions before we look to an elsewhere God to redress the harm we do to one another.

 How do you see the future of religion?

I believe the future of humanity is intrinsically linked with the future of religion. Throughout history religious fanaticism and fundamentalism have wreaked and continue to wreak immeasurable damage upon humanity. I have no doubt that if the Christian, Jewish, and Islamic religions do not overcome their elitist claims to be the "one true religion" with unique access to the Divine, then the future of humanity is bleak. Religion could be the greatest unifying influence in the global community, and yet these three great religions have hardly begun to address the challenge. They are locked into a concept of God that prevents them from affirming the presence of the Divine in all people.

Christians who are moving beyond doctrines that focus on an elsewhere deity, separation from that deity, and who has access to that deity are paving the way for religion to play its rightful role as a unifying influence in the world.

? Do you entertain any hope that institutional leadership in the Catholic Church might one day move in this direction?

The experience of living through the years of Vatican II lead me to be hopeful, despite the backward steps leadership has taken since those years. Catholics in the 1950s could never have imagined the changes that would sweep the Church a decade later. My hope is that whenever the next council convenes it will be forced, because of the movement within the ranks of Catholics and other Christians, to explore the notion of God that will underpin its deliberations. Once that topic is opened for debate, there can be no turning back to outmoded notions of an external deity overseeing the world. Leadership will finally have to deal with the questions and issues we are now discussing.

? What role can or should the pope play in leading the Church into uncharted waters?

It will take a man with the vision and the courage of Jesus to lead the future Church differently — into open and honest dialogue within its own ranks and with the world around it. This is the role a pope should play. Pope John XXIII was such a man, but since his time we have seen the system close ranks and tighten control. Eventually, though, the current system of tight control will disintegrate. It must. The theological schema of salvation on which it depends for its power and authority will not withstand the scrutiny to which it will be subjected in the coming decades.

John Paul II was admired for his vision and courage. However, one devastating limitation — his theology of salvation — led him to adopt an extremely defensive position. This theology dictated his belief that he was God's agent, protecting God's revealed truth — revealed only to the Catholic Church. Faced with the reality that democratic communities no longer give respect to the Church's authority and teaching, the pope resorted to even tighter centralist control within the Church in an effort to win back what was lost. He authorized the Catholic *Catechism* not only as a guide, but as a reference against which to check the orthodoxy of Catholic teachers and theologians. Its theology of salvation is appalling in its outdated understanding of humanity's relationship with God. He appointed bishops who thought within the same narrow theological parameters as himself. He also took away power from regional bishops' conferences and made them subservient to Rome's agenda.

Therein lies the difference between John Paul II and John XXIII. While John opened the windows and trusted the Spirit to blow where it might, John Paul wanted to be firmly in control of how and where the Spirit operated.

Imagine the effect Pope John Paul II could have had — this man of enormous charisma, the man who played the media so well, the man who traveled the world to adoring masses — if he had spread a religious message of inclusiveness. What might he have achieved if he had promoted an end to religious elitism and had given the lead by recognizing the presence of God's Spirit in all people and in all religions — whatever their shortcomings? Instead, operating from what he would have perceived as fidelity to the "truth" revealed only to his Church, he gave the world *Dominus Iesus,* a declaration of the Catholic Church's claim to unique access to God.

 Prior to becoming Pope Benedict XVI, Cardinal Ratzinger had a reputation for strictly enforcing traditional Catholic doctrine. What is likely to characterize his reign as pope?

Pope Benedict XVI, when he was head of the Congregation for the Doctrine of the Faith, articulated a strong stance against "relativism," which he thought reduced the uniqueness of Jesus' role as Savior of the world. He made clear his dismay at secularism and the lack of belief, especially in Europe. He knows the Catholic Church has become irrelevant to many baptized Catholics and is no longer an authoritative voice for them. His reign as pope is likely to be characterized by clear, consistent, and strong emphasis on Jesus' unique role as Savior and on the Church's participation in that role.

Having chosen this ground on which to stand, the pope faces the challenge of being intellectually honest. This should not be difficult for someone who is both a theologian and pope, but in fact, it is a monumental challenge, one that may be beyond him. He has demonstrated his willingness to ignore accepted scholarly opinion about the interpretation of myth and about the dangers of scriptural literalism. He has chosen to immerse himself in a theological mind-set that literalizes the story of an actual "fall" and constructs a theological schema of "salvation" and an interpretation of Jesus as the "unique Savior" that remain intrinsically dependent on that literalizing.

The pope must know that any public questioning about the supposed "actual event" — the words the Catholic *Catechism* uses of the "fall" — would undermine the Church's traditional teaching about Jesus as "unique savior" and the Church's role in "saving" the world.

The pope has chosen his ground on which to stand. Many cardinals, archbishops, bishops, clergy, and laity choose to align themselves with him as "defenders of the faith." But what a cost this is to the Church at large. Faith that will not consider data or scholarship that questions or shakes its foundation does not deserve to survive. Faith that is dressed up as "certain knowledge" and that permits no one to question its most basic premises and assumptions is intellectually dishonest — and should be named as such. The Church deserves and desperately needs better from its leadership.

 Is there a place for "hierarchy" in a future Church?

Any organization needs structure and good leadership to ensure it functions well. The issue is not whether there should be hierarchy, but whether the hierarchy is doing what it is meant to do. Presently, in the Catholic Church, the hierarchy is locked into medieval patterns of operation and thinking. The Vatican, for all its grandeur, history, and symbolism, is steeped in clericalism, power, isolation from the real world, paranoid defense against the Church's own theologians, and an inward-looking, elitist theological system of belief that breeds hypocrisy and the misguided belief that only the hierarchy can discern the movement of God's Spirit.

We need hierarchy, but it needs to be a system in tune with the preaching and practice of Jesus. There are some simple and obvious tests to see whether members of the hierarchy are motivated by the same spirit that moved in Jesus. Are they removed or shielded from the experiences of ordinary people? Do they display wealth? Do they live and act like princes? Are they open to accountability? Do they encourage lay participation in Church governance? Do they use the power their office grants them to bully people into submission? Are they fearful of change? Do they trust the laity? Are they willing to allow people to make mistakes? Do they speak the language of the people, or do they pontificate as pillars of wisdom who know all the answers?

 If the institutional Church were to change in the way you suggest, what would become its primary objective or reason for existence?

It would be what it should always be: to carry on the ministry of Jesus. If it were to divest itself of the theology that views Jesus as someone who won access to God, it would be better prepared to do what Jesus really did — reveal the presence of the Divine in people. That would be the Church's task: to affirm that presence everywhere, to help people ritualize that presence by means of its liturgy, and to challenge all people to give the best possible expression to it.

This would require significant changes in the Church's official liturgy, especially the language and imagery that permeate the eucharistic liturgy. I love my parish community and want to keep the contacts, but I come out of Sunday Mass feeling frustrated or annoyed — and certainly not at all nourished or affirmed in my faith.

When that is the case, I think we need to be very clear in our minds why we are going to Mass. Is it for the sake of keeping alive the bonds of friendship or maintaining a social sense of Catholic identity or some other important value? Given the restraints on and tight control over official ritual, it is unrealistic to expect Sunday Mass to nurture faith for those exploring new horizons.

It would be important for me to have access to the Church's sacramental system.

Yes, but the present system needs radical renewal. It works well for the institution because it locks people into dependency. It ritualizes dependence on priests for access to

God's presence (Baptism, Eucharist, Matrimony) or God's forgiveness (Reconciliation). That attitude is now being rejected by many Catholics who refuse to be dependent on clerical middle management for access to the divine. They want sacraments, but they want a sacramental system that affirms the divine presence with them, not one that claims to *bring* that presence to them.

Yes, but what do we do when the system we are looking for is not available to us?

You create it by joining with other like-minded Christians in faith-sharing groups that nurture growth in faith and that experiment with ways to ritualize that shared faith. You do not need an ordained minister for this. What you need is personal commitment to *being* the "Body" of Christ and the readiness to ritualize that commitment through gathering around the story of Jesus, breaking and eating bread, and drinking wine.

How do you imagine a parish of the future operating?

It is clear we cannot keep doing what is being done: closing parishes, asking priests to cover two or three parishes, and importing priests from other countries to "say Mass" on Sundays, while Church authorities insist that God will send vocations if we all pray hard enough.

I can visualize a parish whose basic structure consists of small groups meeting regularly to share faith, to celebrate the Eucharist, and to organize neighborhood assistance and social justice activities. Men and women, married or single, would preside at ritual. What is now the parish church could be used for larger community activities and celebrations such as marriages. The equivalent of today's pastor could become the local bishop, someone with theological expertise and spiritual training to oversee the parish groups' growth in faith.

This is not as radical as it may seem. It mirrors the "home" model of the Church of the first centuries. The biggest shift would not be so much the parish structure, but the theology and spirituality that would set people free from being dependent on clergy to celebrate the presence of the Divine with them.

 What about theology? It seems that enormous changes will need to take place.

The Catholic Church has a long tradition of being obsessive about correct theological thinking and of silencing anyone not in agreement with the officially approved theological thinking. Correct thinking replaced being a good neighbor as the test of a "true" Christian a long time ago.

Doctrine and theological thinking have a place in the Church, but they should not be as absolutes. Theology is, after all, concerned with a Mystery totally beyond our human words and images. If we forget that, we create theological idols that come to be slavishly worshiped. Theological thinking must be more open-ended. Trying to fit contemporary knowledge about our universe and the development of the human species into the old wineskins

210

of a third-century theological worldview does not work. Theologians know new wineskins are needed to hold contemporary notions about God, but Rome refuses to allow any room to move.

 There seems to be a huge gap in the Church between the academic world of theologians and people like myself with no theological learning. What can be done to bridge the gap?

The best way to bridge the gap would be to provide places and opportunities for open and honest discussion in language people can understand. This is not an easy task, though, as theological academics generally use highly technical language and are not skilled in processes of adult learning. Theologians are also aware of the watchdog mentality that pervades many Catholic dioceses. Consequently they will not step outside the acceptable theological boundaries and share what they really believe.

The greatest difficulty is undoubtedly episcopal leadership wanting to keep tight control over acceptable teaching in dioceses.

Personal responsibility for one's own development in faith is another key factor in bridging this gap. While acknowledging we are not trained theologians, we can nevertheless take steps to join a discussion group interested in taking faith beyond what we learned at school, especially if the group seeks out some of the excellent resources available in print, tape, or video.

211

There seems to be a danger in this of the blind leading the blind. We need some authoritative sources as reference to test whether we are still "Catholic" or not.

We can imagine asking Jesus what the test of belonging would be for anyone in a community that professes to keep alive the mind and Spirit that moved in him. It is safe to assume that Jesus would opt for what is generally termed "spirituality" rather than theology — that is, a right understanding of our relationship with the ultimate mystery we call "God" and a willingness to give witness to that relationship by the way we interact with one another.

 But a "right understanding" can come from theology, so we need to take theology seriously.

Of course. But look what Jesus did. He used simple theology (his understanding of what God is like and where we encounter the Divine) for the sake of spirituality (to help people make sense of their lives and to motivate concern for others). His theology was not a controlling theology. His theology freed people. That is the theology we need to explore together rather than theology that protects institutional identity and authority.

 What of the Bible? Will it, should it, retain its privileged role as the authoritative source to which we turn for guidance?

One of the millstones around the neck of the Christian religion is its focus on the past, as if an elsewhere deity broke through into human history for a brief space of time — and then nothing more ever since. In this perspective the Bible has been commonly viewed as God's last word on any topic, and many Christians will continue to view the Bible in this light. In a different perspective, the Bible will be viewed as the divine presence coming to expression through human mediums (some much better than others) at a particular time in history with its own social issues and cosmic worldviews. Whatever wisdom and insights about humankind's relationship with the Divine and with one another are there will be respected, but the Bible will cease to be viewed as an elsewhere God's last word on matters.

If the Bible is to be enlivening, it must be examined side by side with the belief that the Divine is creatively active with us in these times, in the massive cultural and social shifts we are experiencing.

Take, for example, a Church document on the relationship between men and women. The starting point should be the Christian conviction that the Divine comes to expression in men and women and that this expression, with all its different manifestations, must be respected fully and equally. Then people can look back to see whether or not the Bible respects this equality. Where it does, that is highlighted. Where it fails to do so, as is inevitable because of the patriarchal society in which it was written, that also is highlighted — as an attitude Christians are not to hold.

 What this means, in effect, is that we should not read the Bible uncritically?

213

Yes. We should bring the ground on which we now stand about our understanding of God to our reading of the Bible rather than letting the Bible establish the ground on which we stand.

 That is an extraordinary change for us to make!

It sounds extraordinary, but in many ways you have already made it. You no longer believe, for example, that women should be stoned to death for committing adultery. You do not believe that the Jewish people are "God's people" in the exclusive sense the Bible presents them to be. You do not believe in a deity residing in the heavens. You do not believe in a god who keeps an account of wrongdoings and punishes your children or your children's children accordingly. You do not believe in a god who orders his followers to kill innocent women and babies. You do not believe that a woman should not be touched at a time of menstruation.

It is time, then, to stop being apologetic for critically examining and sometimes rejecting the cultural and community views and ideas that shape biblical passages.

 What about an issue such as homosexuality, which the Bible expressly forbids?

Scripture scholars alert us that the few biblical references to homosexuality are usually in a wider context than the sexual acts themselves. For example, the condemnation in Genesis 19 has as much to do with an abuse of hospitality as it has to do with particular sexual activity. The Bible has no adequate treatment of homosexuality. There is no evidence to suggest that any biblical author had even a vague notion that homosexuality could be a lifelong disposition. The few biblical texts have nothing to do with a lifelong, loving commitment. Christians who think the Bible condemns all aspects of homosexual behavior should accept these patently obvious facts. They might then consider the issue as it should be considered. First, by considering contemporary data about why people are homosexual and why it is not at all unique to the human species. Second, by having respect for the divine presence in all people and respecting people's rights to express love according to their particular sexual orientation. Third, by not equating, as so many righteous Christians do, homosexuality with promiscuous behavior.

Catholics could also keep in mind that the Catholic Church has a high degree of systemic double standards operating on this issue. It officially declares homosexual actions to be intrinsically disordered and therefore sinful. Yet it is well known through the corridors of the U.S. Catholic Church that up to one-third of its priests are homosexual. It is most likely that many of them are sexually active, just as many heterosexual priests are sexually active. If Church authority followed through on its blanket condemnation of homosexual behavior it would move to stop any sexually active homosexual priest from presiding at the Eucharist. It will not do so, though. The system would collapse. So it loudly condemns homosexual relationships, and at the same time covers over the fact that the system relies on sexually active homosexual priests (along with sexually active heterosexual priests) to survive.

? What is being said here about considering contemporary data would apply to divorce as well, wouldn't it?

Certainly. Biblical texts can no longer be the definitive norm for handling this issue. To begin with, the Bible is more concerned with a man's rights to put aside his wife than any rights a woman has. The social context today is also vastly different. Ease of travel, communication, ageing, employment, education, social divisions, and the media are just some of the modern social factors that have considerable impact on marriage and family life.

? Yes, but the ideal that Scripture sets should be maintained: a man should love and respect his wife the way Christ loves the Church. That ideal would rule out divorce.

No, it does not. It is an *ideal*. It sets before the community something to strive for. Most couples on their wedding day are full of that idealism. Their marriage is made in heaven! Their love will never end!

The essential difference is between *should* and *must* or *should not* and *must not*. A Christian couple's love for each other should mirror the love Christ has — if you want to follow that thinking about Christ's love for the Church. The marriage should not come to an end. That is very different from Church law that then legislates and binds

Catholics in law: you *must* mirror Christ's love; your marriage *must not* come to an end — and if it does we will punish you with our Church law: we will deny you Communion if you marry again without an official Church annulment of your first marriage.

The reality is that love between a couple can come to an end. In not accepting this reality, Church authority removes itself from engagement with everyday living and loving. It is not surprising that it is then perceived to be legalistic and lacking compassion by people who put a broken marriage behind them and marry again. We know such people. They are not sinners. They are not cheats. They are loving people who want their marriage to work.

? This is but another example of Church authority being out of touch with the reality of married life. I think *Humanae Vitae* destroyed the trust and confidence of many Catholics.

Church sociologists point to the late 1960s as the time of one of the greatest shifts ever in the Catholic Church. Generally, Catholics of the 1950s were trusting of Catholic Church authority and accepted rather uncritically what that authority decreed. Their acceptance of the dogma of Mary's "assumption" into heaven illustrates that.

The contraception issue, however, impinged on personal relationships, the struggles of married life, the expression of love. People had a personal stake in this issue. They had much to say to Church authority about the joys and the difficulties of sexual activity in a marriage relationship.

217

They came to expect in the Vatican II era that they would be listened to. Vatican II's fine words of a "Universal Call to Holiness" were still ringing in their ears. The Spirit, they had been assured, was released in their lives and in their loving through baptism. And then they found to their dismay, not that the pope did not hear their voice, but that he heard it in the findings of a commission set up to advise him on the matter, was moved by it, and decided to ignore it. He ignored it because he did not want to go down in history as the pope who changed the Church's clear teaching on an important issue.

Worse followed. Church authority in Rome did its best to make the pope's encyclical on contraception an "infallible" statement. The vast majority of Catholics, however, had decided they would no longer abide by a pope declaring: I say so; you must obey unquestioningly. They instinctively knew the early Christian tradition of leadership, "I listen, I learn, I teach," is the only worthwhile leadership style in matters deeply involving people's lives.

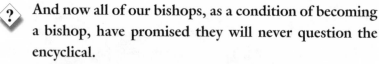 **And now all of our bishops, as a condition of becoming a bishop, have promised they will never question the encyclical.**

That promise compromises the role of a bishop. His role is not to listen — whatever pretense is enacted — but to tell Catholics what the Church teaches.

That happens again and again. We get asked to participate in diocesan assemblies. We pool our collective

thoughts and wisdom, and again and again we are told, "No, you cannot do that.... No, we cannot do that." You wonder why we get asked to participate when all along there are these set boundaries in place, and we are not allowed to think outside them.

This brings us back again to the fact that some of the changes we seek will not occur until the theology that sets those boundaries in place is openly questioned. Priests and bishops are generally reluctant to have such discussion in diocesan or parish assemblies for fear of division erupting between "conservatives" and other Catholics, but it would seem worthwhile to explore people's usage of the word "God" and what they are imaging God is and how God operates.

 What can be done to prevent movements for reform in the Church from stagnating?

Reform movements in the Church will never progress as long as those movements can be blocked by people exercising power and control given to them by the traditional theology of salvation. A requisite for genuine reform is the naming and articulating of the outdated theology underpinning the situation needing reform. This process needs far more attention from people engaged in reform movements. Reformers must educate people into different thought patterns about God, Jesus, Church, and their own sacredness. They have to demonstrate — in the shifts in which people find themselves — that there is other, firmer ground on which to stand and from which to view situations needing reform. They also have to be prepared to stand firmly on that ground and be able, in the face of strong opposition and condemnation, to articulate clearly why they have chosen that ground on which to stand.

An important aspect of this educative process is to help people, most of whom are theologically uneducated, to reflect on some of the basic premises and presumptions of traditional theology, for example, that God is an external deity, that human beings emerged into a state of paradise, or that only through belief in Jesus can people have access to God.

Do you think faith needs to be able to stand up to some rigorous examination?

Yes, adult faith has to go beyond the level of "This is what I was taught to believe, and I trust the people who taught me." While religious faith will always have an aspect of belief beyond what the eye can see, it should be open to rigorous examination of and discussion about the data on which faith is built. It should be open to scientific data about our universe and the emergence of human life rather than using doctrine or deeply entrenched religious beliefs to dictate what data may or may not be considered.

What else needs to be done to help the reform movements?

There seems to be a thin line between loyalty and subservience operating at all levels of the Church. Bishops refuse to stand up to Vatican officials; clergy use their promise of loyalty to the bishop at ordination to justify their silence on crucial issues; Catholics in general think it is disloyal to speak out "against the Church." It all adds up to a system of subservience. The reaction to the sexual abuse scandal stands out because it is such an exception to that system.

Only when Catholics are led to a genuine spirituality that anchors them in the conviction that the Spirit that moved in Pentecost is moving in their lives will that system promoting subservience break down more. So the key issue involves teaching and preaching that affirm the Spirit is with people, ritual that symbolizes and celebrates that presence, and the constant challenge to take responsibility for giving witness to that presence. It is not a Spirit of timidity or subservience.

 I can imagine that the Spirit of Pentecost might lead people in many directions rather than "follow the leader."

We should expect that. The Church of the future must have more respect for diversity, especially in theology and in ritual. The Catholic Church will need to mirror what we want to happen on the global scene: respect for the divine presence everywhere and respect for the many diverse ways this presence comes to expression. The Spirit of our Pentecost will doubtless want to lead people away from thoughts, attitudes, and practices that make them believe they control the divine presence, have unique access

221

to it, or uniquely speak in its name. If the Catholic Church in its own thinking and internal operations does not lead or join other great religions in this movement of the Divine in our times, then religion will continue to be a divisive and harmful influence on humanity's future.

Chapter 11

Model of the Church

I have heard references to Jesus' mother, Mary, as a "model of the Church." In the light of the theological shift we are undertaking, do you think that title has relevance today?

The Second Vatican Council document on the Church, *Lumen Gentium*, cites St. Ambrose's teaching that Mary is "a model of the Church in the matter of faith, charity and perfect union with Christ" (no. 63).

Another Vatican II document on the Church, the Pastoral Constitution on the Church in the Modern World, states that "the split between the faith which many profess and their daily lives deserves to be counted among the more serious errors of our age" (no. 43).

Personal renewal comes from having a spirituality that is able to integrate our Christian faith with our lived experience. Any discussion of renewal in the Church has to move at some point beyond concern for institutional reform and look to personal integration of faith, charity, and union with God. Without this, the Church will never accomplish the task of institutional renewal.

Mary can be a worthwhile model for this personal responsibility for being "Church." For many Catholics, however, the gap between the theology professed about Mary and what happens in their lives is one of the biggest "splits" of all. That split can be bridged only when we free our understanding of her from theology that has made her unreal.

Just as reflection of Jesus would benefit enormously by being grounded in our common human experience and would lead to a more integrated spirituality, so would similar reflection on Mary, his mother. There is much in her life that can resonate with our own lived experiences if we peel away the layers of theology that make her more unlike than like us.

Our difficulty is that we know very little about this woman and cannot take for granted anymore that the Gospel stories featuring her are descriptions of events as they actually happened or that some of the events even happened at all. The accounts of Jesus' birth in both the Gospels of Luke and Matthew, for example, are stories written by people well after Jesus' death to convey to particular audiences a understanding of who the child is rather than biography meeting our contemporary demands for historical accuracy. This is why the stories are so radically different.

Roman Catholic official teaching and popular thinking also make the task of exploring our "common human experience" with this woman difficult. Scriptural literalism and theological reflection grounded in that literalism have demanded that Mary be unlike every other woman in the way she conceived and gave birth. Furthermore, she could not, ever, according to official Roman Catholic teaching, have engaged in the act of love with her husband. And when she died, she was "assumed" body and soul into heaven.

Scholarship and popular thinking in other Christian churches has not been bound and limited by such strict doctrinal limitations. Mary is generally seen as the mother of other children besides Jesus. They are mentioned and named in Mark 6:3. No definitive scriptural evidence is seen for doctrines such as the Immaculate Conception and the Assumption or the belief that she never made love to Joseph. Reflection on Mary does not dwell on titles such as the "Ark of the Covenant," "Mystical Rose," and "Tower of David." She has not been considered as a "mediatrix" between God and ourselves, dispensing God's "graces" to us.

I think many Catholics also do not feel bound to believe in doctrines that make Mary unreal. They try to get beyond them to engage a real woman.

Yes, many Roman Catholics are questioning theological conclusions so out of touch with common human experience, especially the experience of being woman, lover, mother, wife, widow, and elderly woman. It is these experiences they want to engage and reflect on for her to have an impact on their Christian spirituality.

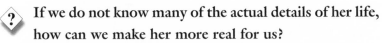

If we do not know many of the actual details of her life, how can we make her more real for us?

One way is to ask, as we consider important times of decision and transition in her life, "What might the human experience have been like?" — using our own experiences as stepping-stones. We can choose to do this in preference to any official demand that we must only think and reflect within the bounds of defined Church doctrine. How was she educated in her Jewish faith? What might it have been like for her as a growing girl coming to terms with her sexuality in a religious environment that placed taboos around menstruation? Did she really fall in love with Joseph? Did she yearn to express her love for him physically? What was her first pregnancy like? If she did have several children, where did Jesus fit in? What was the two-year-old Jesus like? What work did Mary have to do in the village? What might have been her hopes for Jesus?

But we do not know the answer to many of those questions.

That does not mean we should not ask them. Even while not knowing the actual answers, we do know that our reflections make Mary more real to us, and this will be of great importance when we reflect on later events in her life. We are not wasting time or being trivial in using common experiences of growing up — adapting to sexuality, falling in love, marrying and having children — as stepping-stones for reflecting on how life might have been for Mary.

At some time in his adult life Jesus left Nazareth and became a controversial figure. Mark's Gospel, the first Gospel to circulate around the Mediterranean world, presents a family who clearly did not understand what he was about. His own relatives "set out to take charge of him, convinced he was out of his mind" (3:21). Mary is not portrayed well in this Gospel. Later in this same chapter "his mother and brothers" arrive, "stand outside," and send in a message asking for him. It's an interesting scenario. And if Mark were, in fact, our only Gospel, we would be left thinking Jesus dismissed his mother almost completely. "Here are my mother and my brothers," he says, looking around at the people sitting in a circle around him. Mary does not appear again in this Gospel. She is not at the death of Jesus. She is of almost no significance in Mark's story, unless it is in being identified with yet another group of people in this Gospel who fail to understand what Jesus is trying to do. Mark's Gospel is strong in presenting Jesus as a figure of suffering and rejection, constantly being misunderstood and even rejected by people who should have known better.

Other Gospel writers, however, in the light of the impact her son, Jesus, had on people and the way God's Spirit acted through him, wrote her story quite differently. They did so to present their understanding that he was a special "Son" of God, a "light for all the nations," someone who raised the hopes of the downtrodden or a new Moses or the "Word" of God made flesh among us. Her story then appeared in Luke's Gospel with a special annunciation from God's angel, with a pregnancy without male seed to show this was God's work, and a journey to the symbolic place, Bethlehem. Luke's Gospel has angels singing, shepherds — the lowest of the low — present, and Mary uttering her Magnificat giving God praise for extolling the lowly. Matthew's Gospel, on the other hand, has a slaughter of infants, a flight into Egypt, and Jesus going to the top of a hill to preach the Beatitudes, leaving readers in no doubt that there is a new Moses event in this story. Both Gospels use story to highlight the importance of this child to their readers. Later still, John's Gospel presents Mary influential at Cana and faithfully standing by the cross at Calvary.

 Which is the more accurate picture, the earlier one of Mark's Gospel or the much later one of John's?

We do not know. However, if we keep our minds attuned to human experience we may find a way to bridge two vastly differing presentations of the same woman.

If we accept that Jesus was a controversial figure who incurred the hostility of both religious and political leaders of his society, then we may well ask what effect this had on his mother. What stand would she take?

This is a question that goes to the heart and the experience of many Christian families today. Where do we stand when we respect our religious teaching and tradition on the one hand, and yet hear and see our children or grandchildren or someone we greatly respect calling much of what we have been taught to believe and practice into question? What is it like when we find ourselves questioning important aspects of our faith? What is it like to be caught into this tension — something we never dreamed of thirty or forty years ago?

 I recall teaching my children about God and how to pray. I tried to answer all their "Why?" and "How?" questions through their youngest years. I noticed how their questions and attitudes changed when they moved into their teens. I sometimes found myself hesitant and unsure in the face of their questioning. And I found at times their questions and insights made me reflect more deeply on what I believed.

So let us put this common human experience into a house in Nazareth two thousand years ago, and let us imagine the conversations the growing Jesus might have had with his parents and with other relatives, who maybe just started to wonder what this growing lad was up to. We can imagine the insights and questions of the growing Jesus pushing his parents, relatives, and teachers beyond their conventional religious understandings and practices. How come, he might have asked, we profess to be in covenant with God in shaping a society based on God's presence with us and expressing God's compassion, and yet we ostracize the sick and treat them as if God's punishment is upon them? How come we believe God "hears the cry of the poor," yet we treat the poor with disdain? Why do people imagine God is not at all close to them? Why do people fear God's judgment?

The next question is even more dangerous. What are we going to do about it?

Jesus decided to act, and it seems his decision and his actions embarrassed his closest relatives.

Now, if we suppose, going with John's Gospel rather than Mark's, that Mary, his mother, did come around to side with him and support him, we need to consider that she had a struggle on her hands. Here was a woman, a product of what popular Christianity calls "the Old Testament," being challenged to give support to her son in open conflict with religious leaders and with firmly established religious and social practices. Here was a woman being challenged, presumably late in life, to "convert" — to think and act differently. It could not have been easy for her to let go of a lifetime of security, to adapt to change, to side with her son in questions, speeches, and actions that gave scandal to many pious people as well as religious leaders.

It is here that we find the relevance of Mary being a model of the Church for us. It is a pity that the Roman Catholic Church refers to Mary as a "model of Church," yet pays such little attention to how her personal struggle with adjusting to life's challenges can model our own struggles to come to terms with changes, new ideas, and new ways of doing things. This woman could be a model for many of us Christians when we hanker for the old ways, the security we knew, the familiarity with the answers we learned, the absence of tension, the sense that everything was okay in our religious kingdom. This woman's experience of bridging the split between faith and everyday experience mirrors our own struggle. And it can also mirror the experience of many Christians who consider they have moved, prompted by God's Spirit, only to find friends, relatives, and the formal, institutional Church not moving with them. If Mary accompanied Jesus in the years of his public ministry, it may well have been because her relatives and friends in Nazareth gave her as much a hard time as they gave him.

It is not easy to have our well-nurtured religious notions turned upside down. It is not easy to stand outside the comfort zones of our cherished ideas and have them challenged. It is not comfortable being challenged to give reasons for believing what we believe. It is uncomfortable to discover that we have to rethink our stance on some very basic tenets of our religious beliefs. In this context, familiar for many of us, reflection on the experience of Mary takes on a new dimension for us and bears the possibility of acquiring insight and wisdom.

Mary models the reality that adult faith has to be open to new possibilities and to new ways of being expressed and that adults have to be open to unexpected ways for the Divine to move in their lives. Mary did not cling to the old. Mary did not insist that God's Spirit could work only in ways familiar to her. Life demanded extraordinary faith of her in the midst of the upheaval her son caused.

 I often wonder what it must have been like for Mary to stand at the foot of the cross and watch her son die.

Some Christians imagine a woman who was certain her son was God incarnate ("She was told so at the Annunciation"), that the cruelty of her son's death would not have tested her faith in God or in her belief that Jesus' death was for a good cause. They consider she had the comfort of knowing the certainty of the resurrection. However, if we understand the stories concerning the birth of Jesus to be well-after-the-event insight written into accounts of the event many years after Jesus died, we are open to a different perception of Mary at the death of her son. We are open to imagining a woman requiring a much greater level of faith, a faith experience parallel to our own when we confront cruelty and tragedy.

Pain and tragedy can disintegrate our thinking as well as our peace; they can disintegrate the "strong" Christian faith we have had for many years. It is quite common for people in difficult times finding themselves regressing to asking, "Why did God do this?" or "Why did God let this happen?"

At such times faith is a leap in the dark. The reality surrounding us seems to suggest strongly that we believe in a gracious divinity in vain if this turmoil and pain are what we receive in return for our belief. It really is, for many people, the defining moment of true religious faith: what do we believe about the Divine and our relationship with this ultimate mystery when our peace and tranquility are shattered? How can we believe in a generous and gracious divinity when life can be so cruel to us?

Jesus had to face questions like those in the hours and minutes leading to his death. It is hardly likely that his mother, witnessing the cruelty and injustice of his death, would be untouched by the questions that make deep faith an anguishing experience at times. It is at such times of grief, questioning, and temptation to despair that the human spirit has to reach deep inside and in spite of the circumstances of life to proclaim: but I will believe in the power of love and goodness to triumph over all this! I will not give up my faith in the presence and power of the Divine no matter what suffering I am confronted with! That is faith tested by life. That is deep faith. It is ultimately the true test of an integrated Christian faith. Neither Jesus nor Mary was spared the test in their own lives. Life will not spare most of us, either. Life, not an elsewhere God, does the testing. And in the testing it will help us greatly to realize that Jesus and Mary have walked in our shoes and knew the pain of the human condition.

Loss and death are two of the most powerful influences on personal disintegration. We all know people who have never recovered or adjusted following the death of someone close to them. Obviously the reasons for this have much to do with personality and particular circumstances. Fearful religious beliefs also play their part. On the other hand, religion can and should be an important positive factor for Christians in the adjusting and recovering process. The question is whether religion could do more for people before they experience loss and death as well as helping them to adjust afterward. The focus on an integrated spirituality suggests it could do more.

An integrated spirituality would focus, as we have seen, on owning the pain rather than avoiding it. It would help people use their own pain as an instinctive bonding with the human experience of Jesus, the person at the "heart" of their Christian religion. It would help people experience that their pain is shared with him as someone who knew what it is like. It would help people reflect on the Jesus who kept going, in faith, despite life tempting him to despair.

The key word here is "instinctive." None of this will happen overnight. It certainly will not just begin to happen at the onset of tragedy. No, people have to be led to this. They have to hear this Jesus preached to them. They need to hear again and again, week after week, sermons that link the human experience of Jesus with their own experience. Only then will Christians be nurtured into this instinctive bonding with Jesus. Only then will the "split" be healed.

This bonding with Jesus will not work wonders for all Christians in time of pain. However, it is such an obvious help and such an important part of Christian spirituality that its lack of attention in some churches Sunday after Sunday highlights the inadequacy of preaching that teaches rather than resonates with life.

Similarly, bonding with Mary can also help. Here again, though, there are elements of human experience we rarely hear about from the pulpit. In addition to Mary's need to integrate faith with lived experience, with new knowledge and insights, there are four other elements that could help many people immensely in the adjustments life demands of them.

The first is Mary's experience of death. Her husband died and her son, Jesus, died at the peak of his life. What might it have been like for her to go home knowing her husband would never be with her again? And if Joseph died before Jesus began his public ministry, how might she have missed discussing with him the scandal and hostility Jesus was creating in Nazareth and elsewhere? What was it like for her to go "home," wherever that was, when Jesus died? What was that first night like?

Is this the woman we instinctively know? Do we have a sense that she would understand what it is like to be a widow and a mother suffering enormous pain through the cruel death of a son? Do we have a sense of hearts touching in compassion and understanding and minds meeting with questions wrestling about faith in God's loving presence? Do we sense she knows what utter loneliness is like? If we do not, our Christian religion has deprived us of one of its greatest resources for helping us to integrate life and faith.

Second, and this is rarely mentioned in Roman Catholic circles, she aged. In the time and culture she would have been an elderly woman when her son died. The Roman Catholic imagination, bolstered by doctrines protecting her from the normal human condition, is accustomed to a perennially young woman. However, it is most likely she worked very hard all her life and had much wear and tear to show for it in her later years. Interesting, isn't it, that we do not think of her as perhaps needing a walking stick, her eyesight maybe deteriorating, her memory not as good as it used to be, or not being able to do the simple tasks she once could do so easily? There is a theological reason for this: Mary, being free from original sin, would not suffer the effects of that sin such as the deterioration of her physical condition. It is the same theology that demands that the birth of Jesus had to be miraculous — a "virgin birth" — to spare Mary from any pain.

Elderly people could find resonance with many of their lived experiences, the happy and the painful, in prayerful conversation with Mary, "model" of the Church. She could and should be for many Christians one of their greatest resources for integrating their experience of ageing with their Christian faith. Mary has been there. She knows what it is like. But have Christians been led to really know this woman in this way?

Third, and acknowledging we are now into conjecture, we can imagine the presence of this elderly woman in the post-Pentecost community. Her active ministry days were over. She had put in her many years of active service. She was now retired. But what sort of presence was she in and for this young community? It is a bit hard to imagine her telling the apostles things were better off in her young days when everything was black and white and there was none of this confusion and new ideas all around. No, we can imagine she was a woman of great serenity and great trust and as such was an enormous help to a community trying to find its feet. We can imagine the apostles coming to her and relating stories of their ministry and her responding by telling them to keep trusting in God's Spirit.

Fourth, we can imagine her presence in this bustling community as a contemplative one. This is not "contemplative" in the sense of rarefied prayer, but contemplative in the sense all of us are called by life and by Christian faith to be and to pray as we age. Jewish people have a long tradition of this type of prayer: remembering. It is quiet prayer that recalls the past, calling to mind and naming the presence of the divine in the events and people of our lives. We recall and savor and dwell and are thankful. We do this so that we are strengthened in the now of that divine presence and strengthened in the promise of life always in this presence. Any Christian community powered with this type of contemplative prayer in its midst is blessed indeed. We can imagine how blessed the early Christian community was with the presence of this elderly woman urging its members to walk boldly, not timidly, with the power of the Divine at work in them. It is a message we could personally and collectively do well to hear from her today.

I appreciate the comment about prayer, yet I wonder if Mary's prayer life was ever thrown into such confusion as ours. My experience is that having shifted from the notion of God that I carried most of my life, my prayer life has been thrown into chaos. I find myself asking: Is God listening or am I just talking to myself? Does God need my prayers or my worship? It was easy and simple with my old image of God. God heard my

prayer, and He was grateful for my worship. Now I am more confused than ever about prayer!

Yes, there is quite a difference, isn't there? Our notion of God is quite significantly different from the one Mary had. And the questions you find yourself raising are probably not Mary's questions.

What we do have in common with Mary is that like her we are living through a time of enormous shift in our religious understanding. It is important to keep that in mind. She lived through a shift that would have been as momentous to her as ours is to us. She, too, probably needed to articulate, as we have, ground on which she would stand as she lived through it and was not thrown into utter confusion by it.

With the prayer, though, there are similarities worth keeping in mind. Mary's prayer sought to keep her in touch with the God active in her life, the God who did wonderful deeds in her lowliness. We can still pray that. We can still pray, "Behold, the handmaid of the Lord," not in the sense of acquiescence to an external deity, but in the sense of opening all we are to the influence of the Divine within us. We still need quiet times to deepen our awareness of that presence — and to give thanks, as Mary did, for the wonder of who we are.

 So the aim of the prayer is the same, though the manner of it might change?

Yes. The aim of the prayer is to deepen awareness of the presence of the Divine in us, being grateful for it, reflecting on its influence in our lives, and being courageous to give generous expression to it.

The manner of the prayer might change. For example, it can be a sobering and wonderful experience to contemplate the evening sky and think of the billions of galaxies, and then to think that here on this little planet, here in the human persons we are, the Divine comes to expression, and we can be aware of this! We can delight in it. We can use it to give meaning to who we are and what it means to be a human person.

We Christians ought to nurture this awareness of who we are, for it is surely the foundation on which to lay a worthwhile Christian spirituality. It is solid; it inspires; it challenges; it sets us free from chasing the sacred elsewhere and trying to win, buy, or earn an elsewhere God's presence or approval.

If we get wrong the understanding of who we are, then it stands to reason that every subsequent layer we use to shape our personal spirituality and our understanding of what prayer is will lead us astray and create difficulties for us. If we believe we are "exiles" from God we will pray like people who imagine that God is elsewhere and that humankind needs someone to bridge the gap for us. We will also fail to meet the challenges of being the presence of the Divine in our world. We will pass that responsibility on to others whom we consider to be holier and more heroic than ourselves.

Religion can also promote a wrong understanding and tell us that this is not who we are, that we are presumptuous if we think we are close to the Divine. Religion can also mistakenly insist that the presence of the Divine in human beings is restricted to people of a particular ethnic group or religion. Religion can be elitist and exclusive in its claims to have access to the Divine. It can be dominated by attitudes and practices that give specially trained and chosen people special power to bring the sacred to us, creating a religious system of dependence on middle management.

Religion can and still often does miss the point: this presence of the Divine is universal. It is not confined to any group, people, or religious affiliation. The task of religion is not to bring the sacred to us. Its task is to identify, name, and affirm the sacred already in our midst and call us to give witness to it by the way we live.

So we need to develop a prayerful attitude to life that honors the presence of the Divine everywhere and in all people. And personally, we need to cultivate a prayerful attitude to life that leads us to wonder, amazement, appreciation, and gratitude.

If we do this, future generations will thank us for rectifying "one of the more serious errors of our age." Reflecting on Mary's experience of being open to and trusting the Spirit of God can help us achieve the task we set ourselves.

Chapter 12

A Prayer for All People

We acknowledge
a Power, a Presence,
beyond our human words and images,
energizing,
holding everything
in connectedness and relationship,
a Presence
that comes to expression
everywhere˙
at all times
in the vastness of this universe.

We acknowledge
we live and move and have our being
in this Presence.

We rejoice
in our conscious awareness
of this Presence
and of our intimate connectedness with it.

Mindful
of the slow development

of the human species,
we give thanks
for men and women
throughout the centuries
who gave this Presence expression
in the ways they developed
human relationships,
communities
and cultures.

We give thanks
for all men and women
across the centuries
who have struggled
with words and images
to understand
this Mystery
beyond all words and images
and to understand
our relationship
with this Mystery.

We give thanks for
the diversity
of stories and myths
that has allowed people
in different cultures
in different places
in different times
to walk and live in

reverence,
wonder,
connectedness,
and hope.

We give thanks especially
for men and women
who have recognized
the universality of this Presence
and who have called on people everywhere
to nurture awareness of this Presence
and to allow this awareness
to impinge on all our interactions.

We want to redress the harm done
by those religious ideas, attitudes, and actions
that have promoted
superstition
and dependence
and those that have been
divisive and ruinous
elitist
fundamentalist
fanatical
closed-minded
discriminatory,
and violent.

We accept the challenge
to heal the wounds of division

and to respect diversity
as we respect what unites us:
the great commandment to do unto others as we
would want done to us.

As we seek respect for ourselves — we pledge to give
it to others.
As we seek compassion for our shortcomings — we
pledge to show compassion to others.
In seeking forgiveness for our faults — we express
our readiness to forgive others.
In wanting to protect ourselves from violence in
words or deeds, we steadfastly refuse to be
violent in any shape or form to others.
In yearning for respect for our ideas, we will strive
to respect differences of opinion.
In acknowledging our desire to be listened to, we
will strive to be better listeners.
In wanting peace in our lives, we will work for peace
in our world.

We want our belief in the Presence common to all
of us
to be greater than the religious doctrines and
differences that divide us
and we long for all religious-minded people
to share this determination with us.

We want to give the best possible human expression
of this Presence

in our world
so that we and all like-minded people
might establish
a human community
characterized by
genuine concern for all people
in word
and in action.

We pray for our Church
as an institution
desiring it to be a light
in our world.
We pray that,
institutionally,
our Church will die like the grain of wheat
to claims of exclusivity
to elitism
and to theology that protects its power and authority.

We pray that,
institutionally,
our Church
might better imitate Jesus
who rejected power, authority, and control
in favor
of being with people in their day-to-day struggles,
wanting to help them appreciate
the presence of the Divine
in their everyday neighborly actions.

We yearn for the day
when Church leadership
will renew itself
in Spirit
and renew confidence in the presence of the Divine
in all of us
as we strive to imitate Jesus
and be the best possible
human expressions of the Divine
we can each be
in our world.

Notes

1. Karen Armstrong, *A History of God: The 4000-Year Quest of Judaism, Christianity and Islam* (New York: Ballantine, 1994), 78.

2. Ibid., 74.

3. *Galileo: Report on Papal Commission Findings,* 1992, cited in Maureen Fiedler and Linda Rabben, eds., *Rome Has Spoken: A Guide to Forgotten Papal Statements and How They Have Changed through the Centuries* (New York: Crossroad, 1998), 171.

4. Thomas Bokenkotter, *A Concise History of the Catholic Church* (New York: Image/Doubleday, 1979), 325.

5. Ibid., 364.

6. Jared Diamond, *Guns, Germs, and Steel: The Fates of Human Societies* (London: Vintage, 1998), 74.

7. Declaration *Dominus Iesus* on the Unicity and Salvific Universality of Jesus Christ and the Church, August 6, 2000, no. 10.

8. Pope John Paul II, *Exhortation to the Church in Europe,* June 28, 2003, no. 6.

9. *Catechism of the Catholic Church,* no. 614.

10. Pope John Paul II, *Exhortation to the Church in Europe,* no. 20.

11. Ibid., no. 21.

12. *Dominus Iesus,* nos. 13, 14, 16, 20, 21, 22.

13. Peter Hebblethwaite, *The New Inquisition? Schillebeeckx and Küng* (London: Collins Fount, 1980), 13–14.

14. Ibid., 24.

15. *Origins* 31, no. 27 (December 13, 2001): 453.

16. Raymond Brown, *The Birth of the Messiah* (London: Geoffrey Chapman, 1977), 527.

17. Jacques Dupuis, S.J., *Toward a Christian Theology of Religious Pluralism* (Maryknoll, N.Y.: Orbis Books, 1997).

18. Pope John Paul II, *Exhortation to the Church in Asia,* November 6, 1999; see nos. 8, 13 and 14.

19. Pope John Paul II, encyclical *Ut unum sint,* May 5, 1995, no. 97.

20. William Johnston, "Break the Chains and Pray Together," *Tablet* (March 16, 2002).

21. Garry Wills, *Papal Sin: Structures of Deceit* (New York: Image/Doubleday, 2000), 7.

Index

Michael Morwood has an extensive background in spirituality and adult faith formation. He is internationally acclaimed for his clear and accessible writing, workshops, and lectures on the need for Christians to reshape religious thinking and imagination. He lives in Melbourne, Australia, with his wife, Maria. His other books include *Is Jesus God?* and *God Is Near* (with Crossroad) and *Tomorrow's Catholic*.

Visit the author's website at *www.morwood.org*.

To contact Michael Morwood for interviews and retreat and speaking requests, please write *editor@crossroadpublishing.com*.

0-8245-1984-1, paperback

crossroad